A SEASON AT·HOME

A SEASON AT•HOME

THE JOY OF FULLY SHARING YOUR CHILD'S CRITICAL YEARS

Debbie Barr

ZondervanPublishingHouse

Grand Rapids, Michigan

A Division of HarperCollinsPublishers

A Season at Home
Copyright © 1993 by Debbie Barr

Requests for information should be addressed to:
Zondervan Publishing House
Grand Rapids, Michigan 49530

Library of Congress Cataloging-in-Publication Data

Barr, Debbie.
　　A season at home : the joy of fully sharing your child's critical
years / Debbie Barr.
　　　　p. cm.
　　Includes bibliographical references (p.).
　　ISBN 0-310-48101-5 (pbk.)
　　1. Motherhood—Religious aspects—Christianity. 2. Mothers—
United States. 3. Mothers—Employment—United States. 4. Mother
and child—United States. I. Title.
HQ759.48.B37　　1993
306.874′3—dc20　　　　　　　　　　　　　　　　　　　　　　　93-2570
　　　　　　　　　　　　　　　　　　　　　　　　　　　　　　　　　　　　CIP

Edited by Bruce and Becky Durost Fish
Cover design by Terry Dugan Design

Printed in the United States of America

93　94　95　96　97　98 / DH / 10　9　8　7　6　5　4　3　2　1

*"To God who accomplishes
all things for me"
(Psalm 57:2)
and to the women of Helpmate*

CONTENTS

Acknowledgments

This book was written with the help and encouragement of many people. I am thankful for each of these friends, and grateful for their support and for their various unique contributions.

For reading the manuscript, in part or in its entirety, and giving helpful feedback: JoAnn Grote, Alene Robinson, Dr. Gary Chapman, Beverly Meyst, Heather Verga, Andrea Bellan, Ruth Moore.

For taking over my car-pool duties and/or providing child care in order to add to my writing time: Jenna Stamper, Lisa Filipponi, Beth Yancey, Sheila Ernest.

For massive doses of encouragement and prayer: Angie Yoran, Beverly Meyst, Linda Magers, Debbie Ballard, Jackie Mackie, Heather Verga, Gail and Rick Cole, Lynn Parsley, Joan Long, Beth and Al Yancey, Ruth Moore, Barb and John Hageman, Terri Kitchene, Lynn and David Hallsey, Chris Barr, JoAnn Grote, and everyone in Guy Hipp's Sunday school class.

For computer advice: Bob Meyst.

For sharing their thoughts and insights about a season at home or about working at home: Mary Howe, Beverly Turner, Mary Bollinger, Karen Coalson, Joe Verga, Rick Cole, Ron Kessinger, and the thirty women who took the time to respond to my anonymous survey.

For inspiring me: Helpmate and the special women who have served as its speakers and teachers through the years.

For challenging me to go further: Sandy Vander Zicht and Lori Walburg at Zondervan.

Introduction: Should You Read This Book?

Should you read this book? I have two answers to that question: yes and maybe. This book is not for everyone. Is it for you? Only you can decide, but here are my suggestions.

Yes. I encourage you to read this book if:

• You are a mother who has already made the decision to be at home for a season of any length.

• You are a parent or an expectant parent trying to decide whether to continue working or to stay at home for a season.

• You feel torn between wanting to be at home and pleasing a spouse who feels strongly that you should work.

• You are especially fulfilled by your work and question whether staying at home for a season can really be all that important.

• You have been thinking things like, "I really wish I could be at home with my kids, *but* . . ." Your circumstances are neither black nor white but a confusing shade of gray. For example, finances are tight but not desperate.

Maybe. If any of the following apply to you, you may feel that a season at home is out of your reach:

• Your spouse is a full-time student.
• Your family is in a financial crisis.
• Your spouse is unemployed.
• You are a single parent.

In spite of these difficulties, maybe a season at home is possible. Take a quick inventory of your feelings. If your curiosity is kindled by this subject, don't be afraid to read this book. God may have placed it in your hands for a reason.

No matter what your circumstances are, remember that God knows all your questions and concerns. If you choose to read on, take God on your journey. He is the God of comfort, the God who provides, and the God who surprises us with possibilities.

PART
ONE

WHY
STAY HOME?

ONE

Paradigms

There is a time for everything, and a season for every activity under heaven.
—Ecclesiastes 3:1

A few months after my son, Christopher, was born, a good friend came for a visit. She was a career woman, married, and childless by choice. We'd had a lot in common during our mutually childless years and had spent a fair amount of time together. But now, as we sat talking in my home, there seemed to be an odd hint of distance forming between us.

It felt uncomfortable, yet it seemed unavoidable: a new chapter in my life had begun. I was a new mother, totally fascinated by my baby and intent on successfully navigating the uncharted waters of motherhood. My childless friend had trouble identifying with my new order of priorities. We chatted for a while, but as the conversation dwindled, she finally asked, "Uh, what do you *do* all day?"

That's when I first felt *those* feelings. Maybe you've felt them, too: The sudden depletion of self-esteem. The urge to apologize for being at home. The desire to defend mothers at home (knowing in your heart that it's a great choice) but not knowing what to say or where to begin.

I certainly didn't realize it at the time, but I think the day my friend came to visit was the day this book began. I needed validation: Had I made a good choice? Was mothering important work? Could my staying at home make any difference in my child's life?

Exploring the significance of staying at home with one's children became a topic of great interest to me. I started reading. I clipped articles from magazines and newspapers. I paid attention to TV programs, sermons, talk radio shows. I got involved in an at-home mothers' support group at my church. There, I listened as other young mothers talked about their at-home experiences. I absorbed what the older, more experienced moms had to say when they came to speak at our meetings.

Gradually I came to realize that the answer to all my questions was yes. Yes, I had made a good choice. Yes, mothering was important work. Yes, my staying at home could make a tremendous difference in my child's life. Over time, a philosophy began to take shape. That philosophy, woven together with interviews, library research, quotes, and thoughtful wisdom from many places is what you are about to read.

If you are either a new or an expectant parent, you may be in the process of forming your own philosophy, perhaps asking the same questions I was asking at that point in my life. If you are a more experienced parent, you may already have a philosophy in place regarding motherhood, working moms, and moms at home.

But no matter where you are in the philosophy-forming process or where you fall on the moms-at-work, moms-at-home continuum, you can relax. The agenda here is a friendly one. Yes, I'm going to try to convince you of some things along the way, but at its heart, this is a book about affirmation, fulfillment, and balance, both in your role as a parent and—however you define it—in your career as well. If that sounds like what you're looking for, stay tuned.

To really benefit from what follows, you'll need to give yourself permission to think a little differently than you may be used to thinking about these subjects. That means trading in an old paradigm for a new one.

PARADIGMS PAST

A paradigm is a model or an example. For our purposes, a paradigm is a role model that typifies a way of thinking and living. Our American cultural paradigms of women's roles—mothering, marriage, employment—can best be illustrated by (and I think largely originated in) the popular media. There are two paradigms, one old and one relatively new, and their messages strongly conflict.

For many years now, Hollywood and Madison Avenue have worked overtime to promote these two contradictory and damaging paradigms. Even though neither is a true portrait of women's lives in the nineties, they remain rooted in our cultural landscape. These paradigms are so stereotypical and flawed that they actually qualify as myths!

The Myth of Mom at Home

There is rarely a magazine or newspaper story written about mothers at home that does not contain at least a passing reference to (1) Donna Reed, (2) June Cleaver and/or "Leave It to Beaver," or (3) "Father Knows Best." The purpose, of course, is to effect powerful mental imagery that links motherhood with the 1950s. And it works. We *see* the bouffant hairdo, the house dress, the apron, the strand of pearls. We *see* the white picket fence, the tidy little house, and June or Donna or Margaret ever busy in the kitchen.

We recognize instantly that our lives and their lives are very different and that we don't have much in common except motherhood. That's exactly the connection we're supposed to make. The implication is that staying home with your kids is about as trendy as June's hairdo. Worse, the biggest problems these TV moms ever faced seem inane by

17

today's standards: who took that slice from the cake June was going to serve at the ladies' luncheon?

It's important to remember that "Leave It to Beaver" and "The Donna Reed Show" were not documentaries! One definition of a myth is any imaginary person or thing spoken of as though existing. These mythical TV moms and their families never existed. Even in the 1950s, these carefully scripted shows were never more than flawed caricatures of real people and real family life.

But electronic imagery, even when fictional, seems real and thus has an amazing capacity to influence. In the fifties, the message seemed positive: this is what women are supposed to be like. But in the nineties, these icons live on as negative role models. The same imagery now connotes a different message: This kind of lifestyle is a joke. Get a life, lady!

The danger of the mom-at-home paradigm lies in the fact that so many women (and men) have been turned off by it. This wholesale rejection of a stereotype is unfortunate because it cheats today's families by cheapening the choice to be at home.

The Myth of Mom at Work

An opposite myth is today's working mother who has it all. This stereotype is best showcased on glossy magazine pages and prime-time celluloid. The dictionary says that "myths usually involve the exploits of gods and heroes." This myth is no exception. The star of the flawed scenario is a fictional creature named Super Mom. This "has it all" woman would never be mistaken for June Cleaver. She's got sharp clothes and a stylish haircut, carries a briefcase, and rarely cooks. She has everything—nice house, nice car, great job, happy family. (It's been marketed as a package.) And who wouldn't want her life? It's very appealing; it's the American dream.

Super Mom can work forty to sixty hours a week at her fabulous job, keep a spotless house, maintain a sizzling romance with her husband, and spend plenty of quality time with her incredibly mature, cooperative children each evening. You will note that Super Mom is immune to burnout; even after all this activity, she's got energy to spare.

Beneath the veneer of this myth, however, things look different. When Super Mom is unmasked the results are disappointing. It turns out she's an ordinary human being who has to operate within the usual boundaries of time and energy. Her house isn't spotless, her husband and kids are not deliriously happy, and Super Mom is tired. Bone weary, to be exact. The truth is, Super Mom can't do it all—no one can.

The danger of the mom-at-work paradigm is that so many women try to emulate Super Mom. In their pursuit of the impossible, mothers and their families are cheated out of time together, joy, and a quality of life that is rightfully theirs.

Two Problems

Like clothing from a fashion model's closet, neither of these two paradigms fit the average woman very well. In one stereotype, the mother at home wears a June Cleaver house dress; in the other, Super Mom wears haute couture. Few of us want to be June; few of us can be Super Mom. It has taken a long time for us to realize it, but we now know: neither paradigm is—or ever was—real. Because they're not real, they don't work in real life. That's the first problem.

The second problem with these stereotypes is the divisiveness they engender. To exaggerate (but not much), the situation is like a sporting event with two opposing teams—the working moms versus the moms at home. Each side eyes the other camp with a mixture of disdain, suspicion, and, if we're honest, envy. Curiously, the grass on the other side of the fence always seems a bit greener, no matter which yard we happen to occupy. Because these stereotypes are often viewed as rigid, one-size-fits-all roles, women feel forced to choose between them. It's an either-or setup that steals our contentment and pits us against one another.

Women at home with their children sometimes feel like relics of antiquity, painfully out of step with the present. The intensity of this feeling varies widely from one geographic location to another, in accordance with prevailing sentiments and the economic climate of the community. But no matter where they live, moms at home hear questions or insinuations like these: Don't you feel you're wasting your education? Have you decided when you're going back to work yet? What do you *do* all day?

The clear, if unspoken, implication is that unlike time spent at a paying job, time spent at home with small children (or big children) is wasted. Without a paycheck, the value of a mother's work seems questionable. Moms at home, along with children in general, have unofficially been assigned a lower status than other members of our society because they don't produce something that can be measured. Even with all the rhetoric about choice, it's clear that in the eyes of some, moms at home have made a lesser choice. These women suffer the indignity of being looked upon as incapable of holding a "real" job. Their abilities and competence are called into question. Emotionally it's a painful price to pay.

Mothers who are employed full-time have a different problem. Their competence is assumed, but their motives are questioned. In the eyes of mothers at home, working moms can seem colder and less concerned about the well-being of their young, vulnerable children. They appear to prefer making money over making a home. They may be considered materialistic, selfish, or greedy by those who favor an at-home role. It may seem that working moms have placed their career ahead of their kids, and uncaringly so.

While they may have that all-important paycheck, many mothers who are employed forty or more hours a week are convinced they've gotten a raw deal. They would much rather be at home with their kids. They may envy women at home, looking longingly at their flexible schedule, comfortable blue jeans, and abundant time with their children. But they work—often for reasons that may not be readily apparent to their detractors—and they endure the emotional pain of being misunderstood and misjudged.

What mothers with paying jobs may not know is that many at-home mothers secretly envy them. They may envy working moms' possessions, their opportunity to be paid (i.e. validated) for what they do, or their time away from the demands of small children. But working mothers may *experience* social distancing from at-home moms that cloaks their envy. Emotionally it's a painful price to pay.

It's fair to say that both groups have difficulty resisting the temptation to judge the other group from afar. Both groups may feel superior by virtue of their chosen path and may heap guilt, envy, and rejection on women of the other persuasion. It's evident that these stereotypical paradigms cut in both directions—and that they hurt all of us.

Clearly it's time for something new. Most of us are eager to exchange both the house dress and the haute couture for something that really fits us—something more benevolent, more freeing, and more realistic. Let's dismiss June and Super Mom from their posts and take a look at a paradigm whose time has come.

THE NEW PARADIGM

The new paradigm for the nineties and beyond is family-friendly. It's also woman-friendly, embodying balance, realism, and flexibility. It successfully integrates three things: a biblical model, the example of nature, and common sense. Here's the prototype.

Stewardship (The Biblical Model)

The Bible tells us that children are a gift from God (Psalm 127:3). Children are to be cherished, protected, provided for, guided, and trained—a lengthy process over which God has permitted parents to preside. Parenting embodies the biblical concept of stewardship. A steward was a manager or superintendent of another's household and possessions. Christians understand that we have been entrusted as stewards over all that God has given us, and we recognize God, not ourselves, as the rightful owner of all we have.

Children are precious gifts on loan to us. They are not owned by us. Our role in their lives is like that of a faithful steward nurturing a garden to its full and fruitful potential. As parent-stewards, we lovingly cultivate, prune, and water the tender plants in our care.

Today's parents carry out their stewardship at a unique point both in history and within our culture. Unlike the generations before us, our generation finds both men and women being given unprecedented opportunities to do and to become almost anything they desire. For women, and thus for mothers, the doors of possibility have swung wide open. Today's mothers can live their dreams and develop their potential in the world beyond their front door. Today's mothers have been given much.

The Bible says that "everyone from whom much is given, of him will much be required" (Luke 12:48 RSV). Ours is a dual stewardship. We are stewards of the gifts and abilities God has given us; we are stewards, also, of the children he has graciously loaned to us. It is not an either-or proposition.

Each of us will one day stand before God to give an account of both our parenting and the use of our talents and abilities. The rules are the same for all of us, and the ground is level. It's not a matter of choosing sides or of being right or wrong. It's a matter of individual stewardship.

Individual stewardship implies diversity, not sameness. It's important to keep in mind that if God wanted us to live identical lives, he surely would have given us identical children, identical finances, and identical abilities and desires. But he didn't. What's right for one woman, what's right for one family, doesn't necessarily transfer to another. That's why judging each other's lifestyles and choices cannot be part of the new paradigm. These choices are strictly a matter between a woman, her family, and God.

Stewardship is a complex assignment for mothers in the nineties. Our unprecedented opportunities must be considered against the backdrop of the economic instability of our day and the society we must equip our children to face. Good individual stewardship requires a careful, prayerful balance of lifestyle issues and right timing.

Seasons (Nature's Example)

Our own bodies teach us that nature is full of pattern, order, and rhythm. Our bodies are symmetrical. Our hearts beat, our eyes blink, and we draw breath, all within predictably rhythmic parameters. We sleep and wake in cycles. Women ovulate and menstruate at regular, pre-set intervals. Human beings develop in a predictable linear order: we crawl, then walk, then run.

The world we live in is orderly, too. The earth rotates, causing the sun to rise and set on a predictable schedule. Tides come in and go out with unfailing regularity. The seasons follow one another in the same order year after year, century after century. All creation seems to mark time, as if keeping pace with some invisible, infinite metronome.

For all the variegated splendor of creation, it is humanity alone that has been set apart as the apple of God's eye. We are his dearest possession. We are the only created beings in which the Spirit of God will dwell. Our lives, like all of nature, by design have seasons and rhythm. Family life too has seasons of its own, which unfold naturally with the passing of time.

The frenetic pace of our society can keep us from recognizing the natural seasons of our lives. We can be completely out of sync with our season-related needs, and those of our families, and never know it. It is possible to function in opposition to God 's intentions for us because, as his premier creation, it is our privilege to make choices. We can choose to override what is natural in a given season of life.

The pressures and skewed priorities of our culture

compel us to rush the seasons of life or get them out of order or overlap them or try to keep them from changing. When we do any of these things, we invite problems and stress for every member of the family. But in God's economy there is a time designated for accomplishing everything he has called us to do and gifted us to pursue. As Solomon, the wisest man who ever lived, wrote: "To everything there is a season, and a time to every purpose under the heaven" (Ecclesiastes 3:1 KJV).

Narrowing the Channel (A Common-Sense Approach)

Understanding the natural order of seasons in human life or in nature helps foster good, faithful stewardship. A farmer, for example, pays close attention to the seasons. There is a proper season to plant, another season to water and weed, and a final season for harvest. Failure to cooperate with nature could mean the loss of crops. An ignorant or foolish farmer might plant too late. Or he might harvest too early or go on vacation just when the crop was most in need of watering. But as a wise and faithful steward, the farmer performs the appropriate task at the appropriate time. He sequences his duties so that each task is done well and in its proper time.

Applying the principle of faithful stewardship—doing something well in its appropriate season—is not always easy when we go beyond agricultural analogies. But many people have discovered a strategy that is of significant help. I first learned it at a writer's conference. My teacher, a successful author, revealed the secret of her success to the class. She said, "It's the narrowing of the channel that strengthens the stream."

She was telling us that if we wanted to become good writers, if we wanted to succeed at our craft, we must make some hard choices. To say yes to writing, that is, to do something well in its appropriate season, would mean saying no to some other pursuits or putting them temporarily on hold. It would mean sequencing our priorities so that we could pour our energy into what mattered the most in the present season of life. It would mean learning to keep our focus on our goal and measuring other things—good things—in the light of our top priority.

I didn't realize it then, but I had been given more than a prescription for successful writing. Through the years I have come to see that this is a principle to live by. All major pursuits that are truly worth doing well in their proper season require a narrowing of the channel in order to strengthen the stream. If we chase too many big dreams at once or stretch our time and energy and resources across too many commitments, we do nothing well. We reap frustration instead of joy.

The New Paradigm: Sequencing

A major premise of this book is that if there is anything worth doing well, it is mothering our children. Likewise, exercising our talents and gifts to the glory of God—whether that means working outside the home or doing something else—is also worthy of our best efforts. But can a woman always do both things well *at the same time?*

Studies have shown that mothers process their work and family roles differently than fathers.[1] Men tend to separate their roles from one another and attend to their various demands *sequentially*. When they are at work, men tend to focus on work-related duties. When they are at home, they function as a dad and zero in on family matters. In contrast, working moms process their roles *simultaneously*.

Throughout the day women juggle back and forth between their work-related duties and their family responsibilities. They wear two hats all the time. In practical terms, this means if there is a problem at school, mom handles it in the midst of the workday. If a child gets sick or is locked out of the house after school or if there is a problem with the car pool, the mother is far more likely than the father to handle the problem at work. It is more likely, too, that mom will be the parent phoning home after school to check on the

children and that she will search for a last-minute replace-
ment when the baby-sitter fails to show up. When one
parent must take time off from work to see that the kids get
to the dentist, it's more likely to be the mother. Most
mothers with full-time jobs have one foot in the office and
the other foot at home; psychologically they are divided.

The younger the child or the greater a child's needs, the
more the commitments of work and family can overlap. In
certain seasons of family life, these commitments compete
for the same reserves of time and energy, making them
highly incompatible. When we try to live out overlapping
roles, it is often at our children's expense.

Might there be wisdom, then, in finding a way for
mothers to sequence their major commitments, much as
fathers tend more naturally to do?

The answer, of course, is yes. Sequencing allows
mothers to narrow the channel and concentrate on each of
life's major tasks in its proper season. It affirms the idea that
both raising children and exercising our talents and abilities
are aspects of our stewardship, but that they are best and
most fully expressed in separate seasons of life, when they
aren't competing.

Sequencing means narrowing the scope of our pursuits
so as to give priority to children when they are young. Then,
as the seasons of life unfold, we expand into other pursuits
gradually, according to the guidance of God. Sequencing
encourages us to put our priorities in order and to arrange
our lives in keeping with those priorities. It allows us to say
"I love you" to our children in the most convincing way
possible: by being there during the season of their lives when
they need the most nurture and physical care. As our
children's seasons change, we move into new seasons as
well. We shift our focus toward other aspects of our
stewardship, such as developing our abilities or simply
adding to the family income.

When we sequence, we can participate fully in each
season of life, enjoying it and savoring its moments without
regret or guilt. Sequencing gives us time to be the kind of

mothers we want to be, and it gives us the opportunity to be—and to become—all that God has in mind for us.

There is something refreshing and freeing about making a firm decision to set aside one pursuit in favor of another. The goal is still in our plans, but it's in line, waiting its turn. The things that matter most to us are no longer in competition. By saying yes to a season at home, we experience a new sense of power. We're not pushed along by the tyranny of the urgent. We don't feel controlled by circumstances or burdened by stereotypical paradigms that assault our self-esteem or our sanity. The decision to sequence frees us to direct more of our emotional energy toward our children.

Sequencing might even free us to accomplish more in the next season of life. Those with career goals can look to the example of some of our nation's most influential women who have employed sequencing with extraordinary success.

Jeanne J. Kirkpatrick, mother of three, is one such example. A professor, a syndicated columnist, and a former U.S. representative to the United Nations, Mrs. Kirkpatrick spent nine years at home full-time and five more working part-time before she went on to her outstanding achievements.

Sandra Day O'Connor, the respected Supreme Court Justice, enjoyed a five-year season at home with her three sons, working part-time during some of those years.

Yet another example is Patricia McGowan Wald. Before becoming Chief Justice of the U.S. Court of Appeals for the District of Columbia, Mrs. Wald spent a decade at home with her five children, then worked part-time for five more years.[2] Many other women have prioritized their children during a season at home and then expanded their horizons with extraordinary success.

A CHRISTIAN VIEW OF SEQUENCING

Sequencing was first suggested as a path for mothers by Arlene Rossen Cardozo. Her 1986 book, *Sequencing: Having It*

All but Not All at Once, proposed a sequence for career women that went like this: stage one, the full-time career; stage two, full-time mothering; stage three, merging career and family. While I applaud Mrs. Cardozo's innovative thinking about sequencing, I also find it necessary to expand upon it in some ways that are important to evangelical Christian women and their families.

Mrs. Cardozo assumes that most women want careers and that most of them will one day return to work full-time. This may be true, but a Christian view of sequencing must allow that motherhood, in and of itself, can be chosen as a career. Those women whose talents and interests are best suited to mothering, and whose best career choice therefore *is* mothering, deserve equal respect and acceptance. Their sequence, however, will look a little different.

A Christian view of sequencing must also allow for something radical—the guidance of the Holy Spirit. When to stay at home, when to go to work, how to balance money and priorities with family needs—God alone can supply the kind of wisdom and direction parents need to make these decisions. The best implementation of sequencing will occur when mothers and fathers are on their knees, seeking God's plan for their family.

Christians have another unique advantage when it comes to sequencing decisions. When a couple (or a single parent) senses that a season at home is a part of God's plan for their family, they can count on God to make a way, when there seems to be no way, and to provide for their material *needs* (not necessarily *wants*) during a season at home. This notion is sometimes scary, and it is always a faith-stretcher. Nonetheless, it is a clear promise of God (see Philippians 4:19 and Matthew 6:25–33). We'll look at this in detail later. For now—don't panic!

By way of encouragement, it is helpful to remember that a season is not forever. And while many families, perhaps a majority, will require two incomes for the long haul, almost any two-parent, middle class family can, with

God's help, choose to forego a second income for a designated season.

A season at home may require financial sacrifice. It may mean delaying major purchases or living creatively on a tight budget. It may require starting a home-based business. Whatever the cost, putting our kids first at the time they need us the most makes sense. The reasons for having a season at home originate, after all, not with the mother, but with the child. The at-home season is a logical and compassionate response to normal, God-given developmental needs that characterize the springtime of a child's life.

Sequencing gives us a way to respond to those needs. It breathes life and realism into the biblical concept of stewardship, making it especially relevant for the nineties. Best of all, it affords us an at-home season, without regrets and without apologies.

TWO

A Season at Home

> *The beginning is the most important part of the work.*
>
> —Plato

Several years ago, people at my church were enthusiastically passing around the book *Concentric Circles of Concern* by W. Oscar Thompson, Jr. One of the things I liked best about this book was the way the author defined love. It was simple, yet profound: "Love is meeting needs." The author's point was that genuine love for Christ is best demonstrated when we are his instruments for meeting the needs of others. This definition of love is especially applicable to the idea of a season at home.

In every two-parent family, both parents are key players in meeting the needs of their children and modeling love for them. Parents model love, in part, by *instrumental* and *expressive* interactions with their kids. Instrumental modeling occurs when parents are involved in setting limits, disciplining, and showing a child how to plan ahead or how to delay gratification. Expressive behaviors include verbal communication, warmth, sensitivity, care-giving, and emotional support. Both parents model both kinds of behaviors, but moms in particular tend to excel at expressive behavior, or nurturing. (This may be because women are socialized differently than men, or it may be due to inherent biological differences, or to a combination of factors.)

Joe Verga, a clinical psychologist, told me, "Nurturing is a crucial element in normal development. It's a crucial element in neurological development. Children that are loved more, handled more, and nurtured more develop more brain cells."

A woman's propensity for nurture in no way implies that mothers are more important than fathers or that every woman nurtures well; it simply means that in general, God gave mothers the potential for making a unique contribution to their children's well-being. Mothers have been called the heart of the family, perhaps because more than any other family member, the mother tends to set the emotional tone of the home.

Children are profoundly influenced by the degree to which their mothers are consistently positive or negative, energetic or tired, involved or aloof, and emotionally warm or cool. The kind of relationship children experience with their mother has much to do with how well their emotional needs are met and figures prominently in the children's concept, or emotional map, of love.

If love is meeting needs, and if the mother-child relationship is a primary template for children's future love relationships, then how a mother responds to her children's needs is of vital importance.

In my opinion, for a long time we've been focused on the wrong issue and asking the wrong question about working moms. The issue isn't employment; the issue is whether a mother's working interferes with her ability to meet needs within her family. The question isn't, "Should mom work?" Rather, we need to ask, "When and if she does work, can the needs of every family member still be met?" As long as the answer to that question continues to be yes, I think mom can do anything she wants to!

FOUR PHASES

Like adults, children have many different needs: emotional, physical, spiritual, intellectual, social. But children's needs vary widely according to age. Because children's needs change as they grow, the concept of "love is meeting needs" takes on new meaning with each developmental stage.

When I think of a season at home, I think in terms of four phases that correspond to certain age-related processes within children. These phases are not of equal length, and each is significantly different from the others. In each phase, prime concerns are the mother-child relationship and the degree to which the mother's physical presence meets a need for the child. The idea of a mother working full-time or pursuing activities that create a similar separation requires re-examination in each phase, always in light of love meeting needs.

Remember, we are not asking the "should" questions (Should both parents work? Should mothers be at home?). The reason for ousting these questions is that they are throwbacks to the old paradigms and imply rigid, one-size-fits-all answers. We must keep the real issue in mind—meeting needs—and realize that this is the heart of the new paradigm of sequencing.

A Christian view of sequencing incorporates the idea that every member of the family counts and that everyone's needs are equally important. But it also recognizes that within every family there are differing levels of need. Younger, more vulnerable members are given priority because their needs are more pressing. The at-home season exists in deference to the urgency and magnitude of the needs of young children.

Expert opinion and research can guide parents in the sequencing process in much the same way a traffic signal guides us safely through a busy intersection. Drivers can choose to venture through an intersection at any time, disregarding whether the light is red, yellow, or green, but it's a gamble. More prudent drivers look for a green light, or at least a yellow one, before making their move. In a similar way, and for similar reasons, the phases of a season at home can be color-coded red, yellow, or green.

Here are the four phases of the at-home season:

1. Red Light (Phase I): Birth to Age One (the essential minimum)

2. Red Light (Phase II): Age One to Age Three (phases I + II = the recommended minimum)

3. Yellow Light (Phase III): Age Three to Age Six (phases I + II + III = the optimal minimum)

4. Green Light (Phase IV): Age Six and Up (the second mile)

As the color code implies, a mother's presence meets different kinds of needs for her children as the years go by. (Again, this is not to detract from the tremendous importance of dads; it simply recognizes the unique importance of mother-nurture to children's emotional well-being.) Once parents understand this, it is easier to design a season at home that is in sync with family needs. Mapping out an overall strategy becomes a prayerful matter of balance, timing, and preference. Sequencing allows each family a custom-made approach, tailored and timed according to their unique combination of circumstances and family needs.

PHASE ONE: BIRTH TO AGE ONE

In the Old Testament when a man and woman married, the husband was exempt from military service for a full year. During that year, according to Deuteronomy 24:5, he was "free to stay at home and bring happiness to the wife he [had] married." Presumably the purpose of that honeymoon year was to see that the marriage got off to a good start.

A "babymoon"—the first year of a child's life—is a time when parents and infants fall in love with each other. Like a honeymoon, its purpose is to get the relationship off to a good start. The parent-child relationship is new, and for the baby, life itself is new, making the first year full of exciting discoveries for everybody. Research has shown that in some very important ways this first year sets the pace for the rest of the child's life.

In the first twelve months of life, babies experience a developmental explosion. Among other things, they

- begin to master body movements.
- begin to learn language.
- learn how to learn.
- begin to explore the world around them.
- begin to internalize messages from others that form the basis for self-esteem and competence.
- develop their basic human capacity for loving others.
- form an attachment bond with their mother or primary care-giver.

This last task, attachment, is especially significant, and a great deal of research has focused on measuring the intensity of this bond. Attachment is an indication of how secure a baby feels, and it can be a predictor of the child's later self-concept and relationships. One way to measure the attachment between mother and baby is a test called the "Strange Situation." In a laboratory setting, babies are briefly separated from and reunited with both their mothers and strangers, creating a "strange situation" for the baby.

In the past, researchers were primarily concerned with how babies responded at the point of separation, when their mothers were replaced by strangers. They observed that babies who had experienced full-time substitute care reacted in the same way as home-care babies. The researchers concluded that surrogate care had no adverse effect on the attachment bond. However, when researchers began to focus more on how babies reacted during the reunion with their mothers, the controversy over day care was ignited.

Attachment

Following a separation, infants were observed to greet their mothers in one of three ways, which researchers classified as follows:

Securely Attached. Babies were pleased to see their mothers. They may have smiled or produced a toy for their mothers to examine. If the babies were distressed, they were able to receive comfort from their mothers.

Anxious-Avoidant. Babies avoided looking at their mothers or may have begun to move toward them but then turned away.

Anxious-Resistant. Babies sought comfort from their mothers but could not be comforted by them. The babies may have cried angrily or with irritation and refused toys from their mothers.

Why should babies' attachment behavior be of concern to anyone? The answer is that children who show a heightened avoidance pattern toward their mothers in infancy tend to display certain negative traits as they grow older. Researchers began to notice this connection about twenty years ago. But the really big news is a more recent discovery. It is now known that the children who seem to be affected most are the ones who are placed in substitute care for *many hours* each week *during the first year of life*.

It is fair to note that full-time substitute care is not the only factor with bearing on the attachment bond. And full-time care by a child's mother does not guarantee secure attachment. Much depends on the quality of the mother-infant relationship: how promptly, warmly, positively, and appropriately a mother responds to her baby largely determines the bond between them. However, extensive substitute care apparently exerts a major influence on the mother-baby relationship.

Important Research

Research is showing that the mother-baby bond in the first year of life is uniquely critical in setting the stage for the rest of a child's life. Expectant parents and parents of babies must not take lightly the cumulative findings about babies and full-time substitute care. Here is an extended sampling of the research done over the last decade.

A 1980 study reported "a significant relationship between work status and attachment classification, especially for those infants whose mothers return to work/school *during the first year of life.* For these infants there is a greatly increased incidence of anxious-avoidant attachment relationships" (italics added). The researchers also suggested that "the routine separations and the stresses associated with the return to work/school reduce the physical and emotional accessibility of the mother to her infant."[1]

In a 1983 study, Pamela Schwartz observed attachment differences in fifty eighteen-month-olds who were kept in day care full-time, part-time, and not at all. She concluded, "More infants attending day care on a full-time basis displayed avoidance on reunion than infants cared for primarily by their mothers."[2]

In a 1985 study of kindergartners and first graders, those who had entered a high quality day-care program as infants were compared with age-mates who began day care after the first year. The results revealed that the early day-care children "were more likely to . . . hit, kick, and push," and were "more likely to threaten, swear, and argue" on the playground and in the hallways, lunchroom, and classroom. Their teachers rated them as more aggressive and viewed them "as less likely to use such strategies as walking away or discussion" to avoid conflict.[3]

In another 1985 study, three-year-old children were observed playing a competitive game with an adult visitor in their homes. When it appeared that the adult was winning, "securely attached children increased their effort, in order to win, and insecurely attached children slowed down—gave up." The authors of the study felt that the securely attached children probably had more "confidence in their capacity to change the potential outcome failure."[4]

In 1987, researchers studied middle class, intact families whose infants were cared for in their own homes by a non-family member while the mother worked. They observed that "routine, daily separations, resulting from a mother's working outside the home on a full-time basis during (at least) the last four months of her infant's first year of life, significantly increase the probability of an insecure-avoidant infant-mother attachment." They felt that the baby experienced daily separations as rejection from the mother.[5]

A 1990 study by psychologist Carolee Howes found that toddlers who had been in low-quality day care as infants were more influenced by their care-givers than by their parents. (Those who entered day care after age one were more influenced by their families.) As kindergartners, the early day-care children were more inconsiderate, more distractible, and less task oriented than children who entered day care at a later point.[6]

In 1991, a study compared two groups of infants who had already been classified as insecure-avoidant. One group had experienced more than twenty hours per week of non-parental care in their first year; the other group had been with care-givers less than twenty hours a week during the same time. Researchers found that in the "Strange Situation" test, the group with a history of more non-parental care scored worse. They whimpered, fussed, cried more, and played with objects less than the group that had experienced more parental care.[7]

Various other studies collectively indicate that day care before age one may predispose children toward temper tantrums, non-compliance, negativism, and lowered enthusiasm when confronting a challenge.[8]

One study which focused on eight- to ten-year-olds found that those who entered day care before age one were more likely to withdraw from the company of others. These same children were found to have higher levels of misbehavior.[9]

Jay Belsky, a Penn State University professor who specializes in child development, told *Fortune* magazine, "There is an accumulating body of evidence that children who were cared for by people other than their parents for 20 or more hours per week during their first year are at increased risk of having an insecure relationship with their parents at age 1—and at increased risk of being more aggressive and disobedient by age 3 to 8."[10] Belsky cited this same data in an article he wrote for the *Journal of Marriage and the Family*, adding that these risks applied to children in "any of a variety of child care arrangements, including center care, family day care, and nanny care."[11]

Love Is Meeting Needs

We live in a curious culture. Across virtually every stratum of society, there seems to be a call to go back to nature. People are into natural foods and natural clothing fibers. We recycle. We're concerned about the ecosystem, rain forests, and the balance of nature. We want to save the whales and protect the other endangered species. We seem to be striving to cooperate with nature. But when it comes to our own species, we fight against one of the most natural things of all: a mother personally nurturing her infant.

We would not think of taking newborn puppies from their mother before they were weaned. Yet we routinely place human infants in the care of surrogates long before they are ready to separate from their mothers. Recent studies indicate that more than half of all married women with children under age one are now employed,[12] mandating varying amounts of surrogate care for their infants.

Our cultural priorities are out of sync with the seasons of life because we've ignored three of nature's clearest cues:

1. The natural ability of a mother to nourish her baby from her own body implies a close and lengthy physical bond.

2. The natural, inborn attachment needs of the baby, which researchers are uncovering, speak to the necessity of sustained emotional intimacy between mother and child.

3. The intense emotion a mother experiences when she begins leaving her baby with caretakers is a natural, unsolicited response from deep inside the woman. (I don't buy the theory that this is a culturally conditioned response. It's too universal. Virtually every mother agonizes, at least at first, about leaving a tiny baby with substitute care-givers. I

believe the purpose of those feelings is to provide protection for the baby.)

Hesed

During the first twelve months of life, a baby's greatest need might be expressed by the Hebrew word *hesed. Hesed* means lovingkindness or faithful love. It is often used to describe God's love for his people. Throughout the Old Testament, *hesed* is a tender word which "stresses the idea of a *belonging together* of those involved in the love relationship" (italics added).[13]

Many new mothers understand *hesed.* They choose a babymoon instinctively, guided by nothing more than a heart full of love. Others make the same choice, with the same heart of love, but with important additional insights. They know that their personal presence at home puts them in sync with some important developmental needs of their baby.

Dr. Burton White, a renowned educational psychologist who has been called America's foremost expert on early childhood, made an interesting observation. He said that full-time substitute care became popular "not in pursuit of a better way to raise babies but rather for a better way to meet the newly perceived needs of young mothers."[14]

Psychiatrist John Bowlby, perhaps the world's most eminent authority on infancy, gave blunt advice to a young, career-oriented mother: "I don't recommend at all that a mother return to work during the baby's first year. What's important is what's optimal for the child, not what the mother can get away with."[15]

It is becoming increasingly evident that babies' needs are often in conflict with the aspirations and goals of their bright, well-educated mothers. But research strongly suggests that during their first year, babies need a full-time mother. Or, if not full time, for as much time as is possible. Certainly, according to Jay Belsky, more than twenty hours a week of substitute care is too much. In a *Time* magazine interview, psychiatrist-researcher Peter Barglow asked rhetorically, "Is the mother by far the best caretaker for the child in the first year?" His answer: "We think probably yes."[16]

During the first twelve months of life, what a baby needs most is mom herself. To exercise the principle of "love is meeting needs" during infancy, mothers must put sequencing into practice. The first year of a baby's life is the essential minimum season at home.

PHASE TWO: AGES ONE TO THREE

While the most critical phase of the red-light season comes to a close with a child's first birthday, various child development experts encourage mothers to continue on with the at-home season for another twenty-four months, if possible. The red light remains on until around a child's third birthday.

Programming for Life

What is so special about the period of time preceding a child's third birthday? Research has shown that this is an extraordinarily formative time. Many of the "programs" we operate from for the rest of life are written during this time. Who we believe ourselves to be and who we, in fact, become, cannot be separated from the influence of the first three years of life. According to Dr. Burton White, the first thirty-six months of life (and especially the period from eight or nine months onward) "are uniquely critical to the growth of emotionally and intellectually competent individuals."[17]

Dr. White has also said, "I firmly believe that most children will get off to a better start in life if they spend the majority of their waking hours during the first three years being cared for by their parents and other family members rather than in any form of substitute care."[18]

Why should this be so? There are at least three very good reasons for extending a season at home for two more years:

1. Like babies, one- and two-year-olds still lack the

developmental readiness for long periods of separation from their mother.

2. During this brief window of time, children have an almost insatiable desire to learn. Parents are uniquely qualified to take full advantage of this opportunity.

3. The abilities and inner qualities which develop during this phase are the ones that make us especially human. These are the very same qualities which are most easily influenced by those who care for the child.

Let's look briefly at each of the above.

Developmental Readiness for Separation. The mother of a seventeen-month-old boy wrote to psychiatrist Ross Campbell asking whether her son could be harmed by the travel which her job required. Dr. Campbell responded:

> There are certain periods of childhood when it is more critical for a child to be with his mother. Research has shown that the most important period is from 15 to 24 months. The next most critical periods are 9 to 15 months and 24 to 36 months. Remember, though, that every period is important in some way to the child's development.
>
> The exact amount and type of risk to the child's overall development is difficult to predict because every child is different. Some children seem more able at the time to tolerate the mother's absence than others. It may be years before you know the full extent of any harm done.
>
> The normal development of their children is one of a parent's most profound responsibilities. Of course, I don't know how necessary your income is to your family. But my overall advice is to take as few chances as possible with something this important while your child is young.[19]

The critical periods Dr. Campbell refers to encompass all of phase two. Research has shown that the strong emotional bond between mother and child is formed during the course of the first two years of life.[20] The mother's physical presence is very important to the child during this time and for the duration of the red-light phases.

Intellectual and Emotional Growth. Toddlers are intensely curious about the world around them. By eighteen months of age, this curiosity turns into a passionate quest for learning. Between the second and third birthdays, intellectual development skyrockets. By the time children are three years old, they have made tremendous strides in many areas, including language, deductive thinking, problem solving, whimsy or humor, and their ability to love.

It appears that the higher mental abilities such as language, deductive thought, creativity, and humor are the ones most easily influenced—for good or ill—by the kind of care a child receives. Observed Dr. White, "Why these particularly human and particularly valuable achievements are considerably more at risk than the more fundamental ones is an issue for biologists and philosophers. All I know as an educational psychologist is that these are the processes which seem to be most sensitive to variations in child rearing practices."[21]

Quality of Care Makes a Difference. Young children learn best through sensory input—what they can see, hear, taste, touch, smell, and experience. They need an interesting environment—toys, books, playground equipment, and ordinary household objects—to stimulate their minds and exercise their bodies.

They also need an adult companion who will serve as their personal guide and tutor. Talking with and listening to this adult help children learn language. Exploring and playing with this person, as well as receiving comfort and encouragement from him or her, enable children to understand many things. With the help of this interested adult, they can learn how to use words to make their needs known, how to make simple choices, how to use their imagination, how to express love, and many other things. But much depends upon the amount of interest displayed by the adult.

According to Dr. Urie Bronfenbrenner, who has long been a recognized expert on child development, "Children need enduring emotional involvement from people who are irrationally attached to them. In plain language, someone has to be crazy about kids. . . . When this need is met, a child has the equipment to live up to his potential."[22] In my opinion, and the opinion of many others as well, this kind of "irrational attachment" is far more likely to come from a child's own mother and father than from a hired care-giver.

Most care-givers have no trouble feeding, diapering, and dressing one- and two-year-old children. But caring for children on a full-time basis involves more than meeting physical needs, because people are more than physical bodies. Their minds, emotions, and spirits also thirst for stimulation and nurture. How children are touched (roughly or tenderly), how they are spoken to (the tone of voice used and the level of interest shown), whether or not they are treated fairly and kindly, how or if they are disciplined—all these things are part of the process of shaping a sensitive, well-adjusted human being.

Pre-verbal children or those still weak in verbal ability can only receive these messages about their worth at the emotional level and in very simple terms. A basic sense of "I'm good" or "I'm bad" is likely to persist through the years and form part of the basis for future self-esteem. No matter how well trained, how experienced, or how highly recommended a care-giver may be, the most important factor remains the chemistry that exists between a particular adult and a particular child. There is simply no way to *purchase* a quality relationship between two human beings.

During this vulnerable period when children are forming foundations for a lifetime, many parents regard substitute care as more of a gamble than they are willing to take. And many families extend the at-home season through phase two for precisely this reason. For those whose circumstances press them to return to work during the second phase of the at-home season, Burton White has suggested this order of preference when seeking a substitute care-giver:[23]

- Best choice: A warm, intelligent person caring for your child in your own home.
- Second choice: The same kind of person giving care in his or her own home.
- Third choice: The same kind of person caring for no more than three children in his or her own home.
- Fourth choice: Non-profit, center-based care, with low adult-child ratio and at least one formally trained staff person.
- Last choice: Care in a profit-oriented center, with the above qualifications.

Three Years: A Pattern?

When I learned how the first three years of life are so profoundly important, it reminded me of another important three-year period. While researching the subject of divorce and children several years ago, I discovered that it takes about three years for a family to go from the point of divorce to the point where they have made a full adjustment to a post-divorce lifestyle. While pondering these vastly different situations, another important three-year period came to mind as well. I remembered that Jesus spent a period of three years training his disciples before he went to the cross. I also find it interesting that the apostle Paul secluded himself in Arabia for three years following his conversion.

Beyond these observations, I have nothing concrete upon which to base my speculation, but I am starting to wonder whether human beings are simply designed by God to absorb significant change or information over a three-year time span.

Whether or not this is true does not diminish the fact that children's first three years lay critical groundwork for the rest of their lives. So important are these years, in fact, that some experts caution parents against placing their children with full-time, substitute care-givers until after the child's third birthday, when children are generally able to tolerate longer separations from their mother.

Psychologist Joyce Brothers spoke strongly on this subject: "Do you believe the studies that say children need their own mothers during the first few years of life? I realize that the economic necessities of life often force us to do things differently than we would like. But when it comes to child raising, I am convinced that a woman should make every possible effort to spend the first three years with her child. It does make a tremendous difference."[24] Dr. Burton White seconds that opinion: "From six months to three years of age, make sure that the majority of the child's waking time is spent in the company of parents or grandparents. Unless you have a very good reason, I also urge you not to delegate the primary child-rearing task to anyone else during your child's first three years of life. Nothing a young mother or father does out of the home is more important or rewarding than raising a baby."[25]

Baby-sitters Give Mom a Break

In healthy families, everybody's needs are taken into consideration. Mom's needs are important, too, and one of the things full-time mothers need most is time off. Babies and toddlers require someone on duty twenty-four hours a day, seven days a week. Nobody has that kind of staying power! All moms need to periodically recharge, both emotionally and physically.

With that in mind, I want to make it clear that none of these experts would discourage regular or occasional baby-sitters. They are not saying that parents shouldn't take breaks from their small children. On the contrary, Burton White strongly advocates this kind of relief after the baby is six months old. "Most parents," he wrote, "do better if they get away from their children periodically for a few hours at a time." This, he continued, "can make the difference between an oppressive child-rearing situation and a very rewarding one."[26] What experts decry is an ongoing lifestyle of long, daily separations between mother and child. An occasional baby-sitter is good for everybody.

A Thousand Days

If we return to the metaphor of a steward tending a garden, the red-light phases are life's springtime—the planting season. These first three years of life are an opportunity for parents to plant roughly one thousand seeds—one each day for a thousand days. The soil in the garden of children's hearts and minds will never be quite as fertile as during these thirty-six months. It is indeed a unique window of time, ideal for "gardening."

The cumulative message from experts such as White, Brothers, Bowlby, and Campbell is: don't delegate this opportunity to anyone else unless you absolutely have to. The privilege of planting seeds in the garden of your children's hearts is part of your stewardship. What is sown during the spring of life will sprout and remain for all of life. So, if at all possible, be there to plant the seed.

In other words, red light!

THREE

Changing Seasons

> Right timing is in all things the most
> important factor.
>
> —Hesiod, circa 700 B.C.

I once heard a radio interview with a psychologist who was also the mother of two grown children. The topic of discussion was, appropriately enough, motherhood. I happened to be driving at the time, so it was a perfect opportunity for me to absorb some maternal wisdom; my small son was content, snug in his car seat on the passenger's side.

As we drove along, I listened for several minutes, interested, but not completely engrossed in the dialogue. Then the psychologist made a statement that grabbed my attention: "Motherhood is not a job. It's a relationship."

My next thoughts were something along the lines of, "Lady, either you had incredibly self-sufficient children or you've completely forgotten what it's like to be the mother of a small child." I figured maybe time had erased some data from the files in her memory bank! The more I considered her pearl of wisdom, the more I realized that this lady had to be out to lunch: If motherhood wasn't a job, then how come I had to *pay* somebody to take my place?

In retrospect, I see the woman's point. She was right: Motherhood is a relationship. But I was right, too. Motherhood is also a job, especially when children are small. In the beginning, motherhood is more job than relationship. But as children grow and the physical demands (feeding, diapering, getting up at night) decrease, a subtle change begins to take place. There is more two-way conversation. More interactive play. More shared, mutually enjoyable experiences. And without notice or fanfare, the balance tips toward the relationship side of the equation, ushering mothers and children into a new era. It's the yellow-light phase of the at-home season.

PHASE THREE: AGES THREE TO SIX

When children are developmentally able to tolerate longer periods of absence from their mother, the yellow-light phase of the at-home season has begun. For most children, this takes place near their third birthday.

A yellow light means proceed with caution. Phase three is a time of transition. We are no longer constrained by the red light of the most critical developmental phases, but the green light has not yet come on. There are some very important developmental hurdles which children cross between the ages of three and six, and while most children tolerate longer separations from their mother very well, they still need and benefit tremendously from her presence. The yellow-light phase can be a time of challenge for parents who must balance financial considerations, educational pursuits, and job opportunities with the best interests of a three- to six-year-old child.

As when driving, a yellow light sometimes signifies that it's all right to move ahead; in other cases, it's wiser to wait. There are many variables and factors for each family to consider. (Remember, there is no such thing as "one size fits all.")

A season at home which is either continued or begun during the yellow-light years can be highly significant in a child's life and highly enjoyable to both parent and child. A mother's presence at home is still important during these years, but for entirely different reasons than those that figured prominently during phases one and two.

A COURSE FOR A LIFETIME

The yellow-light phase is a unique time of childhood. During these years, children are very much in process. Lynn Parsley, a marriage and family therapist in Winston-Salem, North Carolina, told me, "Between three and six is the time when children develop their sense of personal worth or self-esteem, their control of their impulses, and their gender identity. All those things are important for their entire life's adjustment. So those three years are very, very formative. Their developmental tasks and the way they accomplish them in those three years set a course for a lifetime."

Other things are in process too. Verbally and intellectually the ground is still very fertile and receptive. Half of a child's intellectual capacity develops by the age of four.[1] This intellectual development hinges largely upon language abilities, which are increasing by leaps and bounds during the yellow-light years. As with younger children, children during these years experience greatly enhanced language development by interaction with adults who can play a mentoring role. Children who are read to, sung to, and encouraged to converse with an interested adult hone their verbal skills and have fun at the same time.

Spiritually, children are teachable and increasingly perceptive. Preschoolers can pick up a lot about God, church, the Bible, prayer, and Jesus simply through informal observation at home and at church. Especially around the age of five, children may begin to ask questions about salvation. Some are ready to receive Christ as Savior.

Clearly there is a lot going on in the minds and hearts of three-, four-, and five-year-old children.

Mom's New Roles

During the first three years of life, a mother's nurturing, physical presence, in and of itself, meets special needs for children. During the yellow-light phase, the mother's presence continues to be of great importance, but in different ways. The nature of children's need for their mother's presence changes during this time. Her availability now benefits them in two new and different ways.

Security. A mother's presence, even several rooms away, is important because it creates a sense of security for preschool children. The security comes from the knowledge that their mother is always accessible, a safe home base to which they can return at any time for comfort or help. When children are certain of their security, the freedom to explore, to be creative, and to field test life is released within them. The knowledge that they can depend on their mom to be there allows them to become more independent.

Enrichment. The mother who is available to her children during this phase has the opportunity to provide them with enrichment experiences that can set the stage for lifelong learning. During the yellow-light phase, children still learn best through their senses. Touching, hearing, tasting, smelling, and seeing are their best teachers. They know best that which they have experienced with their senses. The more they can experience, the broader their horizons become. Their mission in life is to discover, invert, dissect, and absorb the world around them. Children at home with an involved, creative mom or dad often have vastly different enrichment experiences than those who spend their days in institutional day-care settings.

When their mother is both available and willing to function as children's personal guide and mentor, preschoolers are opened up to the wonder of life. By walking alongside of them and guiding them through new experiences, a mother mediates her children's first exposures to many things. In this way she helps forge for them an enduring template of attitudes about the excitement of learning. They learn that the world is a fascinating place, full of interesting things yet to be discovered.

By fostering exploration and encouraging their eagerness to learn, a mother helps her children grow into confident, competent individuals full of potential for making a difference in the world. This is genuine home schooling and it can occur in countless ways: a trip to the airport to watch the planes take off and land, a hike in the autumn woods, or a teddy bear picnic in the backyard. Almost any field trip will provide positive social, intellectual, or sensory stimulation for children: preschoolers are always learning in the laboratory of life.

Separation: How Much Is Too Much?

Some experts on young children feel that by the age of three, children are ready to separate from their mother for half a day. Others think more is fine. Still others think less is even better. Lynn Parsley believes that three- and four-year-olds can handle "three to four hours, maybe three or four days a week." This is usually the amount of time involved in preschool programs.

Preschool is an experience which most children find immensely enjoyable, as well as socially and intellectually stimulating. Three-year-olds can benefit from preschool, Parsley said, because they "have a real drive toward cooperative play with other children." Four-year-olds enjoy it too, being "very much in need of social interaction." But too much of a good thing can become detrimental. Discussing children who spend longer hours away from their mother, perhaps in full-time substitute care, Parsley cautioned, "Going in at six in the morning and coming home at six at night is just more stimulation than a child needs at that age."

By five years of age, peers have become very important to children. Time spent away from parents and in the company of age-mates is now far less a trauma and more a treat. But readiness for the adventure of kindergarten varies.

Most children are ready by the age of five-and-a-half, but some are better served by waiting until six. Boys especially, because they often lag about six months behind girls developmentally, may benefit by some extra time at home.

Cues. How much separation is too much? How can you tell? During the yellow-light phase, it may be helpful to take some cues from the kids. Children in this age bracket understand something of their own needs and are becoming more skilled at expressing them. Very often, however, young children do not use words to communicate what's going on inside. Instead, children's behavior may be the best indicator of their needs.

Children who are whiny, fussy, irritable, restless, or tuned out may not actually be misbehaving; they may be expressing a need. It could be a physical need: Are they tired? hungry? running a fever? It could be an emotional need: Are they feeling neglected? afraid? angry?

If less-than-desirable behavior seems to be on the increase just as children are spending more time away from home, the experience may be too stressful. The best initial response to such reactions may be to give children time to adjust to their new circumstances. If behavior does not improve or grows worse, parents should reconsider their plans, if possible. The best course of action may be to increase the children's time with mom and/or dad and extend the at-home season a little longer.

Every child has a unique timetable. According to Dr. David Elkind, "It is not separation per se but *too much separation too soon* that is stressful and harmful to children" (italics added).[2] When we prematurely force longer separations than children are ready for, we create the emotional overload known as stress.

SEQUENCING: IS IT TIME?

Many families begin to implement their sequencing plan in small ways during the yellow-light phase, taking advantage of the time their children spend in preschool, kindergarten, or playing with friends at their homes. Mom's endeavors, when confined to the hours the children would be gone anyway, have virtually no impact on the mother-child relationship. This kind of sequencing is invisible, and for all practical purposes mom is still at home full-time.

Larger pursuits, such as returning to school or going back to work either part-time or full-time, may not be so invisible. These more time-consuming commitments launch the sequencing strategy in a major way. When sequencing is a serious consideration during the yellow-light phase, it's time to examine how the potential changes might affect the way needs are met for each family member.

It may be most helpful to consider any potential opportunity in the light of the differing levels of family needs. What are the greatest needs within the family right now? How will a major investment of time away from home by both parents impact these specific needs?

If the mother has been at home for a number of years, the family's greatest need may well be a second paycheck. However, if the family has adjusted to living on one income and can continue doing so, parents may conclude that it is a higher priority to continue the at-home season in deference to the children.

As the ancient Hesiod said, "Right timing is in all things the most important factor." Right timing with regard to closing or modifying a season at home can be difficult to discern. We can find guidance in Scripture by looking closely at one of the Bible's most famous working moms: the Proverbs 31 woman. This energetic and talented woman was involved in a number of pursuits—buying property, planting a vineyard, ministering to the needy, sewing, selling her handiwork to merchants.

But what about her family? How did her work affect them? We can learn three things from the text.

First, while we are not told the ages of her children, we do know that they were old enough to express verbal appreciation for what their mother was doing. Verse twenty-eight says, "Her children arise and call her blessed."

Second, because the children were blessing their mother rather than cursing or complaining, we can tell that this mother's work had a positive impact on their lives.

Third, her husband was obviously proud of his wife and pleased by her contribution to the family budget. He said, "Many women do noble things, but you surpass them all" (verse 29). We can only assume from his superlative comment that the atmosphere at home must have been pretty positive.

With Proverbs 31 as a guide, it may be helpful to think about three general questions when evaluating any sequencing opportunity during the yellow-light phase:

1. Are my kids developmentally and emotionally ready for me to do this? (Hint from Proverbs 31: Can they express a verbal opinion?)

2. Will the impact on their lives be mostly positive? (Hint from Proverbs 31: Would they be blessing you for this choice?)

3. Is my husband comfortable with the opportunity under consideration and supportive of me? (Hint from Proverbs 31: What is he saying? Are his comments optimistic, encouraging, and positive?)

An important context for these questions is the amount of stress your family is experiencing. Today's parents do it all. We care for our own children, maintain our own homes, yards, and vehicles, and earn a living. We have social commitments, church commitments, car pools, PTA, and play groups. Our lives are busier and more complicated than the Proverbs 31 woman and her family ever could have imagined. That's why it is reasonable to factor in the family's stress level when making sequencing decisions.

If family stress is off the Richter scale due to a major, but temporary, setback, such as a death or a move to a new city, why not postpone other big changes for a while? Following such a major change with more change will be a difficult adjustment for young children. The greatest need within the family may be for all members, including preschoolers, to regain their stability. A decision to delay sequencing at this point could be a very good choice.

If your children are still in the yellow-light phase, here are a few other things to consider before modifying or ending your season at home:

1. Consider how the enrichment and security benefits your children have enjoyed at home with you will change. Does it appear that you will still have a significant amount of time to spend with them? Will their time with another family member increase? (This could be very positive.) Will they be cared for at home or some other familiar place?

2. Consider the combined amount of change-stress likely to occur for your children. This includes daily schedule changes, such as waking time and nap time, transportation, child care arrangements, preschool or kindergarten, and parental absence. To what degree will your children's present lifestyle be uprooted? Do your children react well or poorly to change?

3. Consider the importance of the things still in process, such as gender identity. Think about these as they relate to your particular children. Consider their present masculine and feminine role models. Will your sequencing opportunity provide more time with a good same-sex role model, such as dad or grandma? If so, the change could be a plus. Will your children be in the company of the opposite sex exclusively? If so, how much time will their same-sex parent be spending with them?

Obviously there are many other things to consider. How are your children behaving before you make any changes? How does your children's behavior change when with your intended care-giver? Will your children be spending time with younger, less mature children at your care-giver's home? Some questions you think of will be unique to your individual children and your particular circumstances. Ask God for wisdom.

Delaying Change

Many parents who measure mounting financial concerns or exciting job opportunities against these factors and the prospects of substitute care, upon consideration still regard themselves as the best people for the job. To continue a season at home, they re-prioritize their options and delay major implementations of sequencing.

Thirty-six-year-old Sherry has been at home since her daughter's birth, three years ago. Sherry, who did administrative work before her season at home, plans to return to work when her daughter enters school. She remains at home until that time, however, because, she said, "You can never recapture the precious moments you have with your child. You can always go back to work later, but your child needs you now."

Holly, thirty-three, has also been a full-time mom since the birth of her son, who is now four. She told me, "Watching and helping your children grow up happens only once and then it's gone. You can never get that time back again." Paula advised, "Your child will grow up quickly. Then go back into a career and enjoy it without feeling you're divided."

Experts like Terence Moore would probably agree with these mothers' philosophies—but for more practical reasons. Moore, who did a longitudinal study on the effects of day care in London, has observed that if "a mother keeps her child in her own care full-time to the age of five, the child tends early to internalize adult standards of behavior, notably self-control and intellectual achievement, relative to other children of equivalent intelligence and social class."[3]

No Choice about Change

Many families don't have the luxury of choosing whether or not both parents will work. Families in crisis may find that their financial needs are serious enough to require the mother to return to work full-time during the yellow-light phase. If the father loses his job, becomes disabled, is seriously ill, or dies, or when separation or divorce occurs, a mother may have no choice about remaining at home.

Mothers who must go back to work at this point can take comfort in knowing that they were fully available to their children during the more critical red-light phase. It may also be comforting for them to realize that they are not alone. Eleven million preschoolers now have moms who work, and 39 percent of their mothers are employed full-time.[4]

What about Working at Home?

Fortunately, most two-parent, middle class families with preschoolers are not in crisis. But sometimes, even in difficult financial circumstances, there may be options other than a full-time, out-of-home job. Working at home is one such option.

Focus on the Family cites U.S. Department of Labor statistics showing that, of all married mothers with preschool children, about 41 percent are full-time homemakers. Another 20 percent work part-time, either in their own homes for as few as ten hours per week, or out of the home.[5] Clearly the majority of mothers with preschool children—61 percent—have found a way to be present most of the time during the early years of their children's lives.

Many families' objective is to find some way for the mother to make money that does not remove her from home. These are the families who desire the benefits of continuing to have mom at home through both the red- and yellow-light seasons, yet find themselves severely constrained to increase their income. One solution is to establish a home business or find another kind of money-making opportunity which the mother can do at home.

The yellow-light years—ages three to six—represent the first window of time when working at home first becomes a more realistic and practical option for many women. But, like every other aspect of an at-home season, working at home is not "one size fits all." Working at home may or may not be realistic for you during the yellow-light years. Only you and your family can determine what's best in your unique combination of circumstances.

Chapter nine, "Working at Home," is a full discussion of issues related to working at home. It includes excerpts from interviews with mothers who began their at-home jobs when their children were very young. If finances are your most pressing concern as you enter, or consider entering, a season at home, you may want to skip ahead and read that chapter next.

Working at home is a viable alternative for mothers. Certainly this option is preferable to working outside the home when children are small. Whatever the employment possibilities may be, when a family has a choice about whether or not the mother will be employed it is my opinion that a three-, four-, or five-year-old's needs are best met when a mother can concentrate her attention and energy on the full-time job of parenting.

The years from birth to age six, the red and yellow phases together, define the *optimal* minimum season at home. Mothering full-time for this brief season is a choice to narrow the channel in order to strengthen the stream. While this is not always possible, it is the ideal implementation of a season at home.

FOUR

Sequencing

Times change, and we change with them.
—Anonymous

W hen the youngest child in the family enters school on a full-time basis, the green light comes on. This is phase four, or the second mile of motherhood. The green light means that time has brought mother and children further along the job-relationship continuum. The weight now rests squarely on the relationship side of the time line, edging more in that direction each year, as children edge toward full independence and maturity.

Phase four is the last and longest phase, and the one which bestows upon mothers the greatest freedom and flexibility. For most families, the green-light phase is the best time to implement sequencing. Its special challenge is balancing sequencing opportunities with ongoing family needs.

SEQUENCING TAKES MANY FORMS

As we have noted, sequencing can mean many different things. To many women, it means resuming a career or beginning to work outside the home, either full-time or part-time. For those who want to establish a home business, the green-light years are ideal: moms can conduct business during school hours and be available when the kids get home from school. To still other women, sequencing in the green-light phase means further education, volunteering in the community, or embracing new endeavors as a full-time homemaker. During the green-light phase, a broad definition of sequencing might be *commencing with any activity a woman has intentionally deferred until the time her children are in school.*

As we have noted repeatedly, there are no "one size fits all" guidelines for sequencing. Each family's unique set of needs and circumstances will chart the course, in context with each mother's desires and abilities.

The Other Stewardship: Self

Once a mother's youngest child is in school, it may be time for her to re-focus in a major way on her other main area of stewardship—herself. Her talents, abilities, and interests, her education or training, and other things as well may have been functioning at half-throttle or put altogether on hold during the red- and yellow-light phases of mothering. When the light changes from yellow to green, many women greet phase four with eager anticipation. They are brimming over with ideas and plans for the new season or are delighted about finding a job they will enjoy. Other women, however, dread the green light. They shrink back in fear, hesitant and unenthusiastic about the next phase of their lives.

Fear. One woman may simply fear change itself. Another may fear the unknown as she looks to the future. The source of a woman's fear may be one of the old paradigms: she may feel afraid because what she really wants at this point in her life differs from what she believes she should want, in terms of working or being at home. Women whose self-esteem has rested primarily upon their mothering role may fear becoming less important as their children grow more independent.

Fear is a feeling, not a sin. What we do with fear, however, can be pleasing or displeasing to God. The Bible's parable of the talents, found in Matthew 25:14–30, is most instructive at this point. The story goes like this.

A man was about to leave on a trip and called his servants to him. According to their individual abilities, he entrusted them with varying amounts of silver, measured in large quantities called talents. One servant was given five talents of the precious metal. Another servant was given two of these talents, and a third servant was given one talent. In their master's absence, the three servants made decisions about how to handle the talents entrusted to them. When the master got back from his trip, he called his servants to him and asked them to account for what they had done.

The servant who had been given five talents had done some trading which yielded an additional five talents. His master was quite pleased. He had entrusted this servant with five talents and now found he had ten. He said, "Well done, good and faithful servant! You have been faithful with a few things; I will put you in charge of many things. Come and share your master's happiness!"

The servant who had been given two talents of silver had also done some trading which had doubled his master's money. He had four talents to present to the master. The master was equally pleased with this servant, and he responded with the same words of praise.

The servant who had been entrusted with one talent simply gave it back to the master. He confessed that the only thing he had done with it was bury it in the ground to keep it hidden until the master's return. The master was displeased. He called the servant wicked and lazy and reprimanded him severely. Then he took the one talent and gave it to the man who already had ten.

Why had this servant been so unproductive? The answer is found in verse twenty-five. He admitted, "I was afraid."

Fear immobilizes us. It can stifle our creativity. It can blind us to our opportunities. And in the green-light phase of motherhood, fear can turn an intelligent, talented woman into an unfulfilled, unproductive servant.

Trust. The opposite of fear is trust. To make the most of the green-light phase, a woman must be able to trust in the God who unfolds the seasons of her life according to a wise and inherently good plan. Part of this trust is honest acknowledgment of the gifts and desires within her. The green-light phase of mothering and the accompanying decisions about sequencing are ideally a mere outworking of what is inside her, a natural and comfortable expression of who she was created to be. This is the best possible reason for not judging each other's mothering and sequencing decisions. No one else can determine the best use of our time and talents for us. It's a matter strictly between each servant and her Master.

The Choice Is Yours

At Home. Those whose gifts, talents, training, and desires are best suited to a homemaking role may find their greatest fulfillment in remaining at home for the second mile. They may have a thousand and one ideas about how to creatively use their time. Instead of being bored, they are in their element. Because they have freedom and flexibility in their schedule, they can do many things working moms cannot. These are the women who have time to volunteer for school parties and teach vacation Bible school. They can take a meal to a neighbor when a baby is born. They have time to sit with a friend and offer a listening ear during a personal crisis. They can be there at a moment's notice when a child gets sick at school. They can share and receive spiritual nurture in daytime Bible study groups and can shop and run errands when it is convenient, rather than when under pressure.

Kathie, forty-four, is the mother of three sons, ages six, nine, and thirteen. She has been at home with her boys since the oldest one was born and has no plans to return to work. She views her at-home role as her calling in life and is very much in her element as a full-time homemaker. She explained: "I believe that one of the talents that God has given me is to raise children and to provide a haven for my family. If I give my heart to that calling, I will enable my husband and my children to become all that God desires them to be. I cannot honor him more than by succeeding at that."

At Work. But one size does not fit all! Unlike Kathie, other women are bored and unfulfilled at home. Their gifts, talents, training, and desires are best expressed in other settings. They are in their element when they are pitching a new product to a client, diagnosing a patient, or fund-raising for a charity. They may or may not be paid for what they do, but their work expresses who they are and makes use of their abilities.

When a woman's natural expression of her gifts also generates income, the money may meet a family need. A mother's income may fund a savings account for a child's future college education or it may send a child to a Christian school right now. Her income may provide extras, such as a summer vacation for the family, or it may provide necessities, such as car insurance and clothing.

When other family members are elsewhere during the day, if a woman's preference is also to be somewhere else, doing something else—why shouldn't she? I find no particular virtue in occupying an empty house while other family members are at work or school. Our primary call as wives and mothers is to the people we call family, not to a house or to a stereotyped role called *homemaker.* For some of us, continuing to stay at home during the green-light phase is the equivalent of burying our talent.

Tracy, who had been a secretary for many years, began to stay at home for the first time when her sons were older teenagers. Alone during the day, Tracy felt bored and unfulfilled. She concluded, "I guess I'm just meant to work." Before long, she was a working mom (and a happier woman) again.

The Real You. Recent studies indicate that "homemakers who preferred to be employed were more likely than

65

homemakers satisfied with being at home to be mildly depressed and to have children with attention/immaturity problems."[1] Another study showed "that when a mother's experience of her role (as either employed mother or homemaker) is negative, detrimental effects are more likely to accrue to her children and herself."[2]

It seems important that a woman sense the freedom to choose a role consistent with her natural inclinations. Not only will she be happier, but indications are that her children will also fare better. This is one more good reason for ousting the old paradigms.

Deep down, are you a Kathie or a Tracy? Once you know, decisions about how you'll spend the green-light years will become a matter of balancing your abilities and desires with the current needs of your family. Remember, these are decisions only you and your family can make.

If you discover that your desire is to remain at home and if you are financially able to do so, great! If you choose to work full-time for financial reasons or if you sense that the best expression of your talents and abilities is found in working outside your home, great again! However, when a job is your green-light choice, there are other important considerations which you must factor into your decision.

THE YELLOW LIGHT STAYS ON

If there is a subtle danger hidden within the freedom of the green-light phase, it is that school-aged children may appear to be far more self-sufficient than they really are. Well-meaning parents can assume too much, too soon. While a mother is enthusiastically taking off in a new, exciting direction, her children may be thrown off balance by her exodus and may be in danger of skidding off the runway. This is what is happening to Michael, whose family lives near a friend of mine.

Michael's mother had been at home full-time for several years. When Michael started middle school, his mother decided it was time to look for work. She found a job much to her liking but with a very demanding schedule. Mike's mom had always been there to fix breakfast and send him off to school, but because her job requires her presence early in the morning, Michael does not see her in the morning now. Things in general have gotten more disorganized at home, a particular stress for Michael, who has a high need for structure due to a learning disability.

After school, Michael comes home to an empty house, so he often spends time at another child's home. This child's mother (my friend) is at home during the after-school hours.

Recently, my friend has noticed disturbing changes in Michael. He complains of physical problems and seems to be sinking into depression. Not long ago, out of concern, she engaged Michael in conversation. As they talked, it became apparent that Michael's difficulties are related to his mother's demanding job.

That particular day, Michael had gone without breakfast and had eaten only a single slice of pizza for lunch. By late afternoon, he was hungry and had a headache. His mom, he revealed, would not be home to cook dinner either, since she typically arrives home from work around eight in the evening. Michael is distressed by the fact that he doesn't get to see her very much anymore. Moreover, he is worried and depressed because his family seems to be drifting further apart. He expressed envy for the way my friend's family spends time together. His own family never seems to have time to do anything together anymore, he says. Increasingly on his own and desperately wishing not to be, Michael longs for the good old days when his mom was at home.

Michael's mother, to be sure, made a mistake when she took her job. But going to work, in and of itself, was not her error. She simply failed to discern how this particular job would remove her from meeting many of the legitimate needs of her particular family (for example, her unusually long hours versus Mike's disability-related needs). She responded to the green light by unthinkingly charting a course for herself that overlooked some important family needs.

The guiding concept of "love is meeting needs" still applies during the green-light phase. The appropriate concern is whether every family member's needs can be met if a parent takes advantage of a particular opportunity. This is critical during the green-light phase precisely because school-aged children do appear to be so self-sufficient. Physically, they may be able to take care of themselves. Mike, for example, with a little instruction from his parents, might have been better able to meet his nutritional needs. But the greatest need of many kids like Michael may be for intangibles like conversation and emotional support. When families get too busy, these aspects of healthy inter-generational relationships break down.

Too Busy

Some family therapists have begun to observe that a too-busy family may resemble a dysfunctional family of the sort that grapples with alcoholism or another addiction. While there is no substance abuse, the needs of family members may get overlooked in much the same way. Children don't get help with homework. They don't get their baths or get to bed on time. Their nutritional needs may be overlooked. Harried parents may be completely out of touch with the fact that their children are depressed or lonely.

The green-light phase is a family balancing act. According to psychologist Joe Verga, a child's capacity to handle a lifestyle that includes two full-time working parents is "directly correlated with age." Dr. Verga explained, "The older the child, the more time they've had with the maximum amount of support and nurturing, the more the foundation is in place." He feels, however, that there is no ideal time for a mother to go to work. "Once you get into the teen years, it's a whole new set of issues," he said. "Teenagers need somebody who is crazy about them and is there for them and is going to stand by them."

Sequencing

Looking Back on Childhood

When I surveyed mothers at home in preparation for this book, I asked them whether their own mothers had worked outside the home when they were growing up. I found that their experience was evenly divided. Half (fifteen women) had mothers who worked outside the home. Fourteen women had mothers who were full-time home-makers, and one woman did not indicate whether her mother was employed. Most of the women whose mothers had been at home recalled positive childhood memories related to having their mothers at home. Some of those whose mothers worked had positive memories, as well, expressing admiration and affection for their moms.

Kate recalled, "My mother was able to get a job working the hours that my brother and I were in school. Most importantly, she waited until we were both in school before returning to work. I had a wonderful childhood, and I want to give my children the same warm, loving Christian upbringing. My mom was always there when I needed her." Rebecca felt similarly, and shared, "My mother always made sure that we were not shortchanged, by taking quality time with us in the afternoons and weekends."

Said Pam, "My mother didn't go to work until I was ten. Even once she went to work, she was home during the summers. She also had a work situation where she was free to be involved in school and activities. Her still being involved while working showed me the importance of being available to my children in all they do."

The common denominators among women like Kate, Pam, and Rebecca are these: their mothers waited until their children were school-aged before going to work; their mothers were still able to be available to their children, even though they worked; and, perhaps most importantly, the basic relationship between mother and child was positive and nurturing.

Of all the stories women shared with me via their survey responses, Meredith's was my favorite. As she sat writing her answer to one of the survey questions, Meredith made a surprising discovery. She wrote, "Until I answered this survey, I had always considered my mom a stay-at-home mom." When she began to put her experiences in writing, however, she was surprised to realize that, contrary to what she had recalled, during her school years her mother had worked part-time.

Meredith reflected upon her new realization this way: "I believe [my mom] laid the groundwork for our relationship, for my security, when I was young. Having the security that she would be there for me, if and when I ever needed her, was the key, I believe, for remembering her as a stay-at-home mom. It wasn't so much where she was physically while I was at school, but how I felt about her and her love and concern for me when I was away from her."

Because Meredith and her mother shared a positive, nurturing relationship, "obviously," wrote Meredith, "her working outside the home had no negative effect on me." I love the way Meredith summed up her discovery. She said, "More important than being a stay-at-home mom is being a heart-at-home mom—and anyone can have that."

The Other Side. Unlike Meredith, some women I surveyed shared painful or bitter childhood memories of growing up with a working mother. Sandra, whose mother went to work when she was nine, recalled, "When my mom worked full-time, I had to stay in after-school day care instead of coming home to my mom." She remembers feeling "alone, insecure, and uneasy." She wrote, "My grades dropped drastically," and eventually, "my mom had to quit her nursing job, due to the effects her working schedule had on me." Sandra said the one word that comes to mind when thinking back to life with a working mom is *hurt*.

Kelsey, thirty, wrote bluntly: "I hated it! I feel I was a low priority." She related: "After catching a baby-sitter mistreating me as an infant, [my mom] worked nights until I was six. At that time she went back to work during the day. At that point, things in life became difficult. She was always in a bad mood because she was tired. . . . I always tried to do my load . . . and my mom's load around the house, and then I ended up having to comfort her after a day's work. My sister ended up in lots of trouble, pregnant and on drugs at fifteen. I left home for college at sixteen. I feel much of what happened wouldn't have if Mom had cared enough to say no to material possessions and be home for us—at least after school."

Kris said the word that comes to mind when she thinks about growing up with a working mom is *cheated*. She observed, "Maybe it's just a coincidence, but I've never had a close relationship with my mom, and I can't help but wonder if there is a connection here." Shannon commented similarly, "Maybe, looking back, that was why she was always so tired—too tired to have a relationship with me."

Kathie's word was *loneliness*. She recalled: "I came home to an empty house every day after school. My mother (a widow) was at the end of the phone when I called her at work, and the television was my companion. Yes, I did learn to be more mature and responsible than my peers, but the price was that I also had a less carefree, fun, joyful childhood. I had to grow up faster." As a mother, Kathie has chosen an at-home role because "that was a price I didn't want my own children to have to pay."

The Yellow Light Stays On. As these women's experiences attest, when parents have jobs that consistently focus their energies and attention somewhere other than on the family, it can spell trouble. It is vital that at least one parent's job be flexible enough to allow children's needs to be realistically and adequately met. Mothers and fathers must always remain attentive to the impact of their collective choices upon their families. We must periodically re-evaluate how things are going and be willing to change if necessary. Our needs, our desires, and our goals are important. They are important to us and they are important to God. But they are never more important than the needs of our children. That's why the yellow light stays on throughout the green-light phase.

THE SECOND MILE

When children are babies and toddlers, weary parents may look ahead to the school years with anticipation, knowing that when children can sleep through the night, bathe, dress, feed, and amuse themselves, parental duties will be greatly diminished. Many parents are therefore surprised to discover that the second mile is often the harder mile along the road from cradle to college. Physically, the child is more independent. But emotionally, intellectually, socially, and morally, there is an increasing need for quality parenting. School-aged children do not need less parenting; they need different parenting. Observed one mom, "I have always believed totally that being at home until a child went to school was the best choice. As each of my children has begun school, however, I have seen the need to be at home change, but not disappear."

Ongoing Needs

Kids need someone to care about how their day went and whether or not they do their homework. They need to discuss moral and spiritual values with adults who both care about them and have established good moral and spiritual values of their own. They need to talk about goals for the future and everyday problems. They have decisions to make about friendships, drugs and alcohol, music, and sex.

At every age, whether they are first graders or high school students, children need parental involvement, including, to varying degrees, all of the following:

- companionship
- discipline
- education (about moral and spiritual issues)
- emotional nurture and caring
- guidance
- limits
- love
- protection
- supervision

A Problem. One of the hard realities of the green-light phase is that a parent has to be present, at least part of the time, in order to carry out these functions. I first thought about this while reading Ross Campbell's book *How to Really Love Your Child.* According to Campbell, children primarily perceive love, not in what parents say, but in what they do. To feel loved, Dr. Campbell wrote, kids need four things from their parents: positive eye contact, focused attention (or quality time), loving touch, and discipline.[3] I can't think of a better way to implement the idea of "love is meeting needs" than to speak the language a child understands best—actions, delivered in person, with love.

The problem parents face in working full-time, however, is a narrowed window of opportunity for demonstrating their love "up close and in person." Parents can't make eye contact over the phone. They can't enclose a hug in a note on the refrigerator. And the only way to discipline effectively or spend quality time with children is to be with them.

Family-Friendly Work

Being at home as much as possible during the hours kids are at home seems to be the best solution. But that means finding a family-friendly job. While the pendulum is beginning to swing in a direction more favorable to families, society is a long way from a real solution. The mommy-track idea has generated much discussion but relatively few actual changes in business and industry.

Many companies want to be perceived as family friendly, but in their concern for the bottom line, they send their employees a double message. The *Wall Street Journal* described such a company. On one day, "executives speaking at a banquet praised their most valued employees for such acts as working eight weekends in a row or flying to Japan on business three days after the birth of their child. The next day, the same executives introduced work-family programs inviting workers to take time off for family needs."

The irony did not escape the employees. Noted the *Journal*, "Given the conflicting messages from the banquet, employees are naturally reluctant to use the programs."[4] Similar stories could be told about many other companies.

Latchkey Kids. Finding a family-friendly job is no small task. It may be the biggest challenge facing moms who wish to or need to work outside the home on a full-time basis. This difficulty is evidenced by the fact that latchkey kids now number in the millions. No one is sure exactly how many kids go home to empty houses, but estimates go as high as twelve million.

To many people, latchkey kids are the watershed issue. Most of the debate about full-time working moms and most of the actual problems center around the gap between the end of the school day and the end of the work day. The problems are significant, as illustrated by the following.

The American Academy of Pediatrics conducted a study on substance abuse with five thousand eighth graders in Los Angeles and San Diego. Half of the children were girls, and half were boys. The academy concluded that those who were latchkey kids, caring for themselves eleven or more hours per week, "were about twice as likely as supervised children to smoke, drink alcohol, and use marijuana."[5]

Another study involving eighth graders was national in scope and polled 24,599 kids. The study, released by the National Center for Educational Statistics, identified common risk factors that can negatively affect school performance. Children home alone more than three hours per day were considered to be at risk academically, and 14 percent of the children studied fit this profile.[6]

About thirty thousand girls under the age of fourteen become pregnant every year. Dr. Charles Wibbelsman, chief of a teen clinic in San Francisco, has observed that "most sex between very young kids occurs at home after school before parents get home." He was speaking of children as young as twelve.[7]

Thirty-four-year-old Wendy, an at-home mother of two, told me: "I find myself mothering the neighborhood kids whose mothers work. They like to stop by after school to sit and talk and smell food cooking. They call me with emergencies too. This week, two strange men banged on the door of the house of three little neighborhood girls (ages six, ten, and thirteen). [The girls] were crying and scared and they called me to come over. I did and the men said they were looking for yard work. Those men had seen the younger girls playing outside—there was not a car in the driveway. It is scary to think about what they might have been planning."

This scenario is, unfortunately, becoming more common. Wendy's conclusion is one that is shared by many: "Kids need their parents at home for protection and to help them feel secure."

Flexibility Is a Must. Until the workplace becomes more family friendly, it is clear that if both parents are going to work full-time, at least one parent must have job flexibility. Without it, children go unsupervised and their needs can go unmet. Flexibility answers ahead of time the sticky questions that all working parents inevitably face: Who will stay home with a child who is sick? Who will be there during school vacations? Who will be there after school?

The Energy Crunch. Even a flexible job can wreak havoc in a mother-child relationship if it wrings a woman physically and emotionally dry. When mom arrives home from work too tired to talk, too tired to cook, too tired to do anything but crash-land on the couch, kids and their needs start falling through the cracks. Working couples need to address these energy and involvement issues as well: Who will have enough energy left at the end of the day to help with homework? Who will see that the kids are bathed and in bed early enough to meet the physical need for sleep? Who will see that meals are nutritious? Who will monitor after-school TV and after-school friends? Who will answer questions, mediate sibling disputes, or give a child comfort and perspective on a bad day's events? Who will say no?

A SEASON AT HOME

THE RIGHT JOB

If a mother chooses to work or must work outside the home, her two jobs—her paid job and her mothering job—need to be compatible. That is, she needs the right kind of job outside the home in order to have anything left for her family at the end of the day. What would such a job look like?

A Mother's-Choice Job

When I surveyed mothers, asking them to tell me what an ideal job would be for them, their responses were (not surprisingly) similar. A mother's-choice job had part-time hours and built-in flexibility.

Most mothers expressed a preference for a workday that began and ended along with the school day. Many said that having a job with flexibility was important so that they could be at home when school was not in session or could leave work to pick up a sick child or attend a school function. Most of the mothers also indicated that they preferred to return to the workplace only after their youngest child had started school.

Holly's comments were typical: "I would like for my children to be old enough to be in school all day. An ideal job for me would be one that would start after I've been able to see my kids off to school, and end so I could be there when they got home. I would like to be off when they are off."

Looking ahead to the day she will return to her teaching career, Rebecca cited one of the advantages of her profession: "I will not work summers. Teaching allows me to have the best of both worlds once my children are in school." Cami, whose training is in television production, also anticipates a workable schedule. Her objective, once her children are in school, is an on-site TV production job with hours from 9:00 a.m. to 2:00 p.m.

Defining It Further. Certainly much depends on each woman and the needs unique to her family, but almost any working mother will cope better if her job

1. does not create an excessive amount of internal

76

FIVE

Eight Good Reasons

You are the bows from which your children as living arrows are sent forth.

—Khalil Gibran

Most mothers who choose to spend a season at home do so with a deep inner conviction that they have made an excellent choice. Yet because the mom-at-home and Super-Mom stereotypes are still alive and well within our culture, a season at home—regardless of its length—often draws criticism. Many parents find it difficult to translate their inner sense of having made a good decision into answers that will satisfy those who question or deride their choice. Toward that end, this chapter is intended as an apologetic.

An apologetic is a defense of a belief, a cause, or a philosophy. An apologetic is not an apology or an excuse. Instead, an apologetic offers reasons, proofs, support, and validation for a position. While this chapter presents an apologetic, it makes no apologies for a season at home.

Whether parents regard the at-home season as a

sacrifice or a dream come true, it is a choice that finds additional support from the following eight concerns.

1. THE PACE OF MODERN LIFE

When I was a college student in the early seventies, I majored for a short time in recreation and parks. This curriculum seemed to hold promise for the future: all indications were that as we pushed closer to the year 2000, Americans would have more leisure time on their hands. People speculated that we would have so much free time that we would be at risk of boredom. We were taught that recreational pursuits of all sorts would become our great national panacea.

But the exact opposite has happened. Americans now work about 140 hours more per year than they did twenty years ago. Figuring in commuting time and fewer days off, our jobs now claim the equivalent of an extra month of our lives each year. A Washington research group reported, "Americans are starved for time. Increasing numbers of people are finding themselves overworked, stressed out, and heavily taxed by the joint demands of work and family life."[1]

Leisure time is shrinking, and family time is shrinking right along with it: parents now spend 40 percent less time with their kids than they did twenty-five years ago.[2] One study found, not surprisingly, that "more than possessions or fancy vacations, children want more time with their families."[3]

There is no longer anything unusual about parents who work fifty or sixty hours a week. In certain fields, such as marketing, law, accounting, and the computer industry, employees are often expected to come in early and stay late. Those who don't are viewed as uncommitted. One father, a former sales manager for a major computer company, claimed he was fired from his job for putting his family ahead of his work. He said his boss told him, "This is not a family company and never will be. . . . It's a disadvantage to be married . . . to have any other priority but work."[4]

Physicians and other professionals often spend long hours away from home or on call. Pilots, sales personnel, and corporate executives log many hours in the air each year. Even when they are at home, ostensibly enjoying some leisure time, voice mail, fax machines, personal computers, and paging devices keep many professionals plugged into their jobs.

When civic and church commitments, school involvement, and obligations to extended family are added to a demanding job, there is little time left for ordinary, garden-variety fun and relaxation. No wonder 50 percent of 1,010 people polled said they would gladly trade a day's pay for an extra day off each week. Contrary to the predictions of the seventies, leisure time is a rare commodity, fast becoming the new status symbol of the nineties.[5]

When one parent has a demanding career, family life can be significantly impacted; when both parents are on the fast track, the cumulative pace and pressure can become unbearable. Many families do not survive. Two-career couples lead the nation in divorce.[6] Many mothers choose a season at home to restore balance, flexibility, and order to family life. Kerri, a mother who traded her full-time nursing position for part-time, on-call work, explained: "I changed hours to get my sanity back. I am a better person now that I can spend more time with my children and caring for my household."

2. DECLINING AMERICAN CULTURE

I opened this morning's newspaper and was greeted with the news that a local fourth grade child took a .32 caliber revolver to school with him this week. This is the fourteenth such incident in our area in the past four months, and these situations have involved high school, middle school, and elementary school students.

The lead article on the same front page was a heartbreaking interview with the father of a sixteen-year-old boy named Aaron, who was killed in a violent, one-car accident.

The driver, another teenager, had been drinking and lost control of her car, slamming it into a tree. She and two other passengers were injured, but Aaron did not survive. Said the dad, "You expect your kids to outlive you."[7]

The parents of these kids will probably spend today wondering what they could have done differently. They may have warned their kids about how dangerous guns or alcohol can be. They may have expressly forbidden them to touch firearms or to ride with someone who had been drinking. But the kids made their own choices, based to some degree, I suspect, on their perceptions of what is cool.

We can thank our culture for instilling kids with such a cool set of values. Parents can and do strive to combat the influence of culture, but it's major, time-consuming warfare. I think columnist Ellen Goodman described it well when she wrote:

> At some point between Lamaze and PTA, it becomes clear that one of your main jobs as a parent is to counter the culture. What the media deliver to children by the masses, you are expected to rebut one at a time.
>
> Are the kids being sold junk food? Just say no. Is TV bad? Turn it off. Are there messages about sex, drugs, violence all around? Counter the culture.
>
> Mothers and fathers are expected to screen virtually every aspect of their children's lives. To check the ratings on the movies, to read the labels on the CDs, to find out if there's MTV in the house next door. All while keeping in touch with school and in their free time, earning a living.
>
> . . . It isn't that [parents] can't say no. It's that there's so much more to say no to.
>
> . . . It's not just that American families have less time with their kids, it's that we have to spend more of this time doing battle with our own culture.[8]

It's a different world out there, compared to just one generation ago. American cultural values have never been more vulgar, more openly hostile to Judeo-Christian principles. The world has entered a new season, characterized by lengthening shadows and the chilly breath of evil. Immoral excesses abound. According to evangelist Jay Strack, one out of every nine teenage girls becomes pregnant. Twenty-three percent of today's brides are pregnant when they take their wedding vows.[9] The list by now is familiar: drugs, AIDS, crime, teen suicide, abortion, child abuse, pornography. Never have kids needed more parental guidance. And never has a faithful, prayerful, available parent been more of a protective blessing to a child. I think it's fair to suggest that, in the nineties, a season at home may be more important than ever before.

3. DAY CARE

While there is much debate about day care and much continuing research regarding its long-term effects, there are two things about day care which are rarely debated anymore.

Quality. Most children in day care are not in situations that would qualify as high-quality care. High-quality care includes:

- Teachers trained in child development or early childhood education
- Low adult-to-child ratios
- A low staff turnover rate
- A developmentally appropriate program
- A clean, safe environment

High quality day care is, in a word, expensive. There is also not enough of it to go around. Most kids, as a result, are cared for by workers who are not the highly touted professionals most parents would hope for. Many children spend their days in the company of undereducated, underpaid, disinterested baby-sitters who know very little about young children. Because pay is low, the turnover rate for child-care workers is high. This is a problem because children need consistency: just as a bond is forming between worker and child, the worker gets a better job offer and quits. The next worker may quit, too. And children learn that the people they care about and depend upon can disappear from their world.

The ratio of adults to children is important because, theoretically, the lower the ratio, the more adult interaction each child receives. An ideal ratio for three- and four-year-olds is seven children to one adult. From the standpoint of cost, however, this is unrealistic. An acceptable rule of thumb is to multiply the child's age by three. Thus, for three-year-olds, a nine-to-one ratio would be good. For four-year-olds, twelve-to-one; for two-year-olds, six-to-one; for babies, three-to-one. Yet ratios greatly in excess of these numbers are common, and care suffers accordingly.

Illness. Day care and illness go hand in hand. It is a well-documented fact that children in group day care experience more illness than those cared for at home. Ear infections, colds, flu, and diarrhea are especially common among day-care children. Less common, but of significant concern, are giardiasis (an intestinal infection caused by a parasite), hemophilius influenza B (bacterial meningitis), and cytomegalovirus. Cytomegalovirus, which displays no symptoms in the children who carry it, is of concern because, if contracted by expectant mothers, it can infect the fetus. Half of the babies exposed to cytomegalovirus in utero will be born with eye disorders and delayed mental and physical development.[10]

Children are especially susceptible to illness between six months and two years of age. For the first six months of life, antibodies received from their mothers before birth provide protection. These wear off, however, and because the immune system takes about two years to fully develop, there is a window of vulnerability.[11] The cost of day care, plus the cost of medication and repeated trips to the doctor during this period can sometimes equal or exceed a working mom's pay.

Many parents opt for a season at home to avoid the emotional and physical risks that accompany day care. Carol told me that one reason she chose to stay at home with her two sons was, "I didn't want my children being exposed unnecessarily to illnesses."

4. THE PITFALLS OF WORK THAT DOESN'T FIT THE WOMAN

Work, in and of itself, does not necessarily cause a woman or her family problems. But there is plenty of evidence mounting to show that when a woman and her job are mismatched, draining her energy and creating stress, problems can be significant.

A recent study suggested: "When a mother is trying to cope with an excessive number of overlapping work and family demands, her concentration and attention will be affected, and she will experience negative moods. Such a mother may be less attentive to her children and adopt less time-consuming and less effective parenting behaviors."[12]

The same study found that the more negative a parent's mood, the more the parent was likely to respond to a child with rejection or in a punishing manner. The researchers noted: "Specifically, the more rejecting the parent, the higher the child was rated on anxiety/withdrawal. The more punishing the parent, the higher the child was rated on conduct disorder and attention/immaturity."

An earlier study suggested that "when people experience stress at work their patience, sensitivity, and responsiveness toward family members may be reduced."[13]

Working women with children, according to a 1991 survey, are "more than twice as likely as men to feel constant stress." Over 40 percent of the women surveyed said they feel trapped by their daily routine.[14] In a separate study, conducted by Hilton Hotels, 35 percent of women surveyed said they were trying to accomplish more than they could handle.[15]

A mismatch between a woman and her job can create intense stress, pressure, and exhaustion. As a result, a mother can become irritable and emotionally distant from her family. She may be less patient and less capable of dealing with children's problems and concerns at the end of the day. Worse, exhausted moms want a hot bath and time alone; they don't want to play with Legos or Barbies. Exhaustion and stress take the quality out of quality time and leave kids feeling isolated and neglected.

Dissatisfaction with the incompatibility of full-time work and family life is widespread. A 1990 survey reporting "major attitudinal changes" shows that the pendulum of popular opinion has started to swing in the direction of home. More women now think part-time work is best for moms, and for the first time in twenty years, less than 50 percent favor a career for mothers. Fifty-six percent said they would quit working altogether if it were financially possible for them to do so.[16]

5. THE MYTH OF QUALITY TIME

Aside from the parental exhaustion factor, the idea of quality time falls on its face for other reasons.

Young Children May Not Be at Their Best at the End of the Day. Even when an adult arrives home from work full of mental and physical energy, it is likely that a young child's peak hours have already come and gone. For many preschoolers, morning is the time when they are most cooperative, energetic, and well-rested. Quality time is diminished or lost altogether when kids are too tired and irritable to enjoy it.

Real Life Cannot Be Scheduled. Life's surprises and disappointments tend to happen spontaneously. A rainbow can't be scheduled. A fall from a swing can't be foreseen. Much of what makes for quality in any relationship is the experience of sharing together whatever is happening in the present moment of life. Scheduled quality time is positive in that it gives the child time with the parent, but it is no substitute for the parent's being there to share the joy or dry the tears. The mother who hears vicariously about her children's day builds a different relationship with her children than the mother who experiences her children's day along with them.

Good News Is Old News By the End of the Workday.
The second telling of the day's events is often not as
enthusiastic as the first. And the first telling usually goes to
the person who is available, whether that person is a baby-
sitter, grandma, or mom. Young children are not oriented to
a clock. They are also not well-practiced at delaying gratification; they tend to live in the present. Thus, by the time
quality time rolls around, what seemed important and
exciting a few hours earlier may now seem like old news.

Maintenance Tasks Often Take All Available Time.
When both parents work, evenings can be hectic. After
work, children must be picked up and errands must be run.
Once home, the family must be fed. After the kitchen is
cleaned up, there are baths to give and homework to do.
There's a lot to accomplish in the space of a few hours, and
even an unexpected phone call or a minor crisis of any sort
can steal the opportunity for quality time. For many families
quality time has turned into "maybe some other time." It
rarely occurs.

6. THE GIFT OF CHILDHOOD

A full-time working mother once told me that she did
not think that her preschooler had been harmed at all by
having been in substitute care since she was a few months
old. She may be right. Certainly, no physical harm was
done, and perhaps there will be little or no psychological
harm either. But after I spoke with this mother, I found
myself wondering whether harm is always the most important issue.

I wondered whether this intelligent little girl had been
adequately enriched and affirmed by her experience. Had
her caretakers delighted in her as a unique and precious
individual? Had they noticed and praised her accomplishments? Had she been encouraged to explore her environment? Had she been disciplined with love or disciplined at
all?

I wondered about her internal sense of self, of her

parents, and of life: was it somehow different for having spent so many waking hours away from her home and family? There is no way to know, of course, but I concluded that while spending one's early years in substitute care may or may not be toxic, it is hardly the stuff from which precious childhood memories are made.

It seems that by divine design, childhood is meant as a time to play, to be spontaneous, innocent, curious, and carefree. Unlike animals, which mature rapidly by comparison, human beings mature slowly, taking many years to reach emotional and physical adulthood. We are vastly more complex, and childhood is necessary preparation for adulthood.

One of the chief benefits of a season at home is that it lets a child unwrap the gift of childhood slowly. When mom stays at home, a child is spared the stress that results from a "pit stop and pajama" lifestyle—a lifestyle that revolves around getting ready to go somewhere. Sleepy, pajama-clad children are often carried right from their cribs and beds to the sitter's. Many don't see their parents again until it's time to put those pajamas back on. Home is often only a pit stop between one day's rush and the next.

But preschoolers whose mothers are at home enjoy the fabulous privilege of getting up in the morning and not having to go anywhere. They can cuddle with mom and listen as she reads a Bible story. They can watch "Sesame Street" in their pajamas or go outside to play with the dog in the backyard. These brief, preschool years are part of the gift of childhood—the only years when children's lives will not be ruled by a clock. School and its schedule and pressures will arrive soon enough. Then comes a lifetime of work— possibly nine to five for the rest of life.

A season at home also lets children enjoy the sense of being special companions to their mother, instead of being one in a crowd. At home with her, they get one-on-one attention. Even when siblings abound, each child receives far more personal attention than in group day care or, when school begins, in a classroom of twenty or twenty-five students.

When mom is at home, there is more flexibility, and less hurrying. Life on the slow track is a good idea, according to Dr. David Elkind, because, "Young children (ages two to eight) tend to perceive hurrying as a rejection, as evidence that their parents do not really care about them."[17]

One major difference between families taking an at-home season and families where both parents work is who is adapting to whose schedule. When a mother is at home, the adult does the adapting. Mom can drop everything, if need be, to respond to a need or to take advantage of a teachable moment. She can stop to look at an interesting bug or to put a Band-Aid on a skinned knee without giving a thought to the clock.

Conversely, when both parents work full-time, the children adapt. They must conform to the adults' pre-scheduled, clock-oriented lives. When both parents must be out the door by 7:00 a.m., there is no time to contemplate the frost on the windowpanes or to put a silly face on Mr. Potatohead. The luxury of whimsical, spontaneous play can't take place Monday through Friday.

A season at home is a deliberate choice to travel in the slow lane, at a child's pace. It is a choice to preserve childhood.

7. THE MOTHER-MENTOR

One afternoon I was talking with my six-year-old son as we sat in his room. In the course of our conversation he mentioned something about a faithful steed. I had no idea where he'd heard this phrase, but I had a hunch he didn't understand its meaning. I decided to find out. I asked, "Chris, do you know what a steed is?"

"No," he admitted.

"Well," I said, "it's a horse. A steed is a horse."

"Oh."

I continued, "Do you know what *faithful* means?"

"No."

"It means that somebody is always there when you need them. That's why we say God is faithful. You can talk to him anytime you want to. He's always there when you need him."

Chris was quiet for a moment. Then he said, "That's what you are."

Know what? As the meaning of my son's words sank in, I felt pretty good about being a full-time mom. And upon reflection, I felt even better about my six-year season at home. It occurred to me that since children learn best through the channel of their personal experiences, the experience of having had what he viewed as a faithful mom would make it easier for Chris to apply the concept of faithfulness to God.

If we had not had that conversation in Chris's room that day, I doubt I would have thought about the possibility of children forming such an experiential link. But it makes sense. Parents are the template from which children create their concept of God. Spiritually, parents are their children's mentors.

Webster defines a mentor as "a wise, loyal advisor; a teacher or coach." I believe that a mother or father's consistent, daily presence fosters spiritual mentoring. Being available, faithful, and involved teaches children more than that their parents care. It also teaches them that God cares.

Deuteronomy 6:6–7 is a prescription for spiritual mentoring: "These commandments that I give you today are to be upon your hearts. Impress them on your children. Talk about them when you sit at home and when you walk along the road, when you lie down and when you get up." These verses indicate that the torch of spiritual truth is passed across the generations deliberately, over a long period of time, and in the normal course of daily life.

When at least one parent has the time to go for leisurely walks down the road, eternally significant conversations can take place. When a parent has time to sit around the house and chat with the kids, truths are passed on as interest is piqued and questions come up. At bedtime, at breakfast time, and at unpredictable times during the day, spiritual mentoring—discipleship—can occur.

Jesus trained his disciples by living his life before them. He ate with them, walked and talked with them, and took them along when he raised the dead, fed the multitudes, and healed the sick. That kind of constant discipleship has no counterpart in modern society. But the closest parallel I can think of is the twenty-four-hour-a-day relationship shared by an at-home mother and her "disciples." Children understand true Christianity to the extent they experience it in their own families.

A mother-mentor influences her children not only spiritually, but intellectually, emotionally, and creatively as well. The Gallup Organization once compared the childhoods of extraordinarily successful people with the early years of average people chosen at random from the general population. The results of the survey, published in *Family Circle*, showed that the super-successful were reared by parents who

- practiced encouragement, but not intellectual prodding.
- valued spending time with the child over spending money.
- frequently engaged their child in conversation and discussion.
- supplied their child with many interesting books.
- made sure that dad, as well as mom, took an active role in the child's life.[18]

Good mentoring also involves fostering independence in children, giving them responsibilities, showing them affection, and treating them with respect. Being at home maximizes a mother's opportunities for mentoring her children's creativity, curiosity, talents, and interests. Studies have shown that moms at home "have roughly twice the amount of direct contact with their children compared to employed mothers."[19]

Let me hasten to say that, with regard to mentoring, home is not so much a place as it is a sense of connectedness between parent and child. In that sense, the idea of staying at home with one's children can be misleading if taken literally. The real significance of a season at home is not found in a particular geographic location (such as the home), but in being with one's children.

Part of mentoring is exposing children to life, to ideas, to culture, and to nature—expanding their horizons. So, as long as mother and children are at the museum or the library or the zoo or the park *together*, they are at home. And because home is the relationship they share, not the address, mentoring can and does occur almost anyplace.

8. CHILDREN ARE MEANT TO BE ENJOYED

In addition to all the positive things children experience when their mothers are at home, there are many nice things that accrue to moms and dads as well. One of the chief benefits for mothers is the opportunity to establish strong emotional ties with their children. Many women also discover to their satisfaction that full-time mothering cultivates and fine-tunes their feminine capacity for nurturing.

Beyond these things, many mothers count simply being able to be at home their chief blessing. Karen Coalson, a work-at-home mom, gets excited when she talks about the advantages of being able to work at home. She said, "It's been real meaningful to me. I mean, I can't believe that I've gotten to share my children's childhood with them, that I was able to stay at home and share stuff with them, instead of working until five o'clock."

Presumably, one of the reasons couples have children in the first place is so that they can experience the joy of raising them. From first words, first steps, and first teeth to first dates and first jobs—these are joys God intended for parents to experience. When we delegate the daily care of our kids to others, we also delegate much of the joy that rightfully belongs to us as parents. A season at home means that *you* get to have the fun and emotional satisfaction of watching your children grow up, one day at a time. As a parent, the joys belong to you. Why give them away unless you have to?

SIX

No Higher Calling

Where did we ever get the idea of "just" being a mother? In the Bible, when God wanted to do something special for a woman, He gave her a child.

—Charles Stanley

In the third chapter of Genesis, God made some assignments to Adam and Eve just before they were banished from the Garden of Eden. To Adam, God assigned the task of earning a living. The Bible uses words such as *toil*, *thorns*, and *sweat* to describe the effect that the curse of sin would have on Adam and his work. To Adam's wife, God assigned the task of bearing children. Sin's fallout on women meant that childbearing would become a painful ordeal. Adam then named his wife Eve, which means "life giver."

As descendants of Adam and Eve, we inherit both their assigned tasks and the accompanying curses. Today, however, couples collaborate on their assignments of working and parenting a great deal more than our first parents did. Collaboration between husband and wife is essential to a successful implementation of sequencing.

Through the years, this collaboration goes through

95

several adjustments. Ideally, it works like this: When children are born, the husband and wife collaborate through a division of labor which places priority on the children. As the head of the family, the husband helps his wife nurture their children by financially supporting the family without her help. In this way, he affords his wife a season at home and gives priority to her assigned task from God. This foundational time is an investment in the future stability and emotional well-being of the children and in the health of the family unit as well. Fathers who are willing to collaborate in this way not only provide for their families economically, but also emotionally.

As children grow and the seasons of family life change, the couple adjusts their strategy. As they assess their family and their finances, they may determine that the wife's season at home can be modified or brought to a close. It may be time for the wife to help her husband with his assigned task. As his helpmate (Genesis 2:18), she now works with him to increase the economic base of the family.

ETERNAL PERSPECTIVES

Bearing, raising, and providing for children is a calling with job descriptions written by God himself. As such, parenthood could not have a more noble status in the eyes of God. With regard to motherhood in particular, Dr. Charles Stanley said, "A woman is never more than she can possibly be before God than when she is being a godly mother and a godly wife."[1]

Mothers at home have a job that entails the privilege of working with an eternal commodity: human beings. Money, houses, cars, status, position, education, fame, and all else this world has to offer will one day come to an end. They are temporal commodities. People, on the other hand, will live forever.

A season at home, and all it requires in time, energy, and resources, is a wise investment in the light of eternity. But holding onto an eternal perspective is sometimes difficult. When the baby has diarrhea, the dog is chewing on the furniture, the kids are fighting, and the doorbell is ringing, it's hard to remember why you're doing what you're doing. Yet while stretching and stressful, raising children is definitely—and eternally—a worthwhile investment.

Moms are only human, of course, and under stress we can lose perspective and become discouraged or depressed. Most mothers at home, at least occasionally, question the importance of their work and battle with poor self-esteem.

For those mothers in the throes of battle, the February 1993 issue of *Focus on the Family* magazine carried a wonderful bit of encouragement on its back cover. A man named Wayne Bohke took the time to write this letter of encouragement about moms at home:

> Back in September, you published a letter from Darcy Neal-Croteau of Quebec, who talked about battling the low self-esteem she was feeling as a mother of preschoolers. She should consider the following:
>
> As a driven and determined product of a family of modest means, I set the goal of becoming vice president of a Fortune 500 company by age 35. On the way, I earned a full academic scholarship, became a U.S. Navy officer, earned two degrees in engineering, supervised hundreds of people, and finally reached my goal at age 34.
>
> I could have risen much higher in the corporate world, but I opted out at age 40. In the meantime, my college-educated spouse raised our three children. It was not that I ignored them, but 12 hours a day at work and graduate school at night left limited time.
>
> I am now 56 years old, the children are grown and successful, well-adjusted people, and guess what? The business I worked for has been acquired twice over, and no one in the company even remembers I was there.
>
> The point of this letter is to encourage you and the other mothers of preschoolers and grade schoolers to hang in there and continue to do the world's most important job. And if your self-esteem suffers as you change yet another diaper or wipe a dirty nose, just re-

read this letter from someone who has seen the supposedly "important" jobs from the inside; being a mother carries much more responsibility and influence than any company vice president will ever experience.

Mr. Bohke's letter, besides stimulating my gratitude, brought two thoughts to mind. First, it reminded me of the famous quote from William Ross Wallace, who lived during the 1800s: "The hand that rocks the cradle is the hand that rules the world." Mr. Bohke's letter struck me as a more modern version of the same thought. I like the fact that two *men*, living in different eras, affirmed the profound influence a mother can have.

Second, Mr. Bohke's letter called to mind another contemporary bit of wisdom: In retirement homes, aging business tycoons and corporate executives do not regale their visitors with tales of their most brilliant career accomplishments. Instead they pull out cherished, dog-eared pictures of their children and grandchildren and boast of *their* accomplishments.

Wall Street investment superstar Peter Lynch (whose savvy was behind the astoundingly successful Fidelity Magellan mutual fund) didn't want to wait until he got to the rest home. In recognition of what really matters to him, he walked away from a multi-million-dollar income to spend more time with his wife and three daughters. He said, "I don't know of anyone who wished on his deathbed that he had spent more time at the office."[2]

When all is said and done, it is relationships, not possessions or accomplishments, that bring us the greatest satisfaction and joy.

PARENTS ON THE ROAD LESS TRAVELED

Many parents agree philosophically that a mother's influence can be profound and that children are vastly more significant than anything this world has to offer. The idea of a season at home is very appealing to these parents. Convinced of its merit, they would truly love to set aside a window of time for nurturing their children at home. But they regard a season at home as something they can't afford to do, a luxury out of reach. As most any mom currently at home can attest, the mere suggestion that one might consider quitting work to stay home tends to strike fear in the hearts of many working parents. But dual-income couples are invariably curious. They want to know, "How do you manage to do it? How can you possibly afford it?"

In an effort to fully address those questions, I decided to let some parents in the midst of a season at home speak for themselves. Beginning in this chapter, and continuing throughout the rest of the book, they will share their reasons for choosing a season at home and their strategies for surviving successfully on one income.

I asked the thirty mothers in my survey to explain why they thought it important to be at home, what kind of sacrifices they've made in order to stay at home, and what advice they would give to other parents trying to decide about a season at home. Their response was enthusiastic. These at-home moms were glad for the opportunity to elaborate on one of their favorite subjects, and they were eager to share their thoughts and experiences. Many took the time to write pages of additional, thought-provoking commentary, full of heartfelt perspectives and personal anecdotes.

To get a male perspective, I interviewed some fathers at length: What were their thoughts and feelings about having their wives at home for a season? What would they tell other dads currently weighing the pros and cons of life on one income? What did they fear? How did they believe a season at home could benefit their kids or help them be better dads?

At first glance, this group of parents appears vastly diverse. Educationally, they range from high school graduates to those with advanced degrees. Some are, or are married to, professionals—pilots, physicians, business people. These families live comfortably, and the parents get frequent breaks by hiring sitters. Others in this sample are, or are married to, blue collar or clerical workers. These families live more modestly, affording the luxury of a baby-sitter only occasionally. Yet, setting economics and education aside, this group of parents actually forms a very homogeneous group: they share a unity of heart.

The common priority of these men and women is family first. In their comments, these parents exuded commitment to their children. Women expressed gratitude toward their husbands for supporting their desire to be at home; men expressed appreciation for their wives who were parenting full-time. As a group, they viewed a season at home positively, confident of the value of the investment—and sacrifices—they are making.

Why We Chose a Season at Home

The reasons for choosing a season at home are as varied as the backgrounds of the parents making the decision. The men and women in my sample group gave many different reasons for their choice.

Dee, thirty-eight, said that she simply "did not want someone else to have all the fun of watching my children grow up." Sherry, the mother of a three-year-old, said, "I wanted to be the one to influence my child's life, to be the one to see all the 'first time' things, and to be the one to meet all of her needs." Kate was concerned about the influence other care-givers could have on her children: "I saw my children taking on the ideas, attitudes, and values of their day-care workers—some good, some bad."

Tara's reasons surprised her. She had planned to return to work as a medical secretary after her baby was born, but she says she "never knew how much I'd love that baby until I had her." Unlike Tara, Holly had always cherished the idea of being at home. "Ever since I can remember," she said, "I knew that when I had children, I wanted to be at home with them as they grew up. I could never envision myself placing my children in the care of someone else while I went off to my job." To Holly, staying at home was a goal so important that, "it affected every major decision that I made," including her choice of a college major, a spouse, and an affordable home.

For some, years of personal observation played a role. One mother recounted: "I used to see a lot of children due to the nature of my work. I was a dental hygienist. I noticed that the children whose parents had decided that the mom would stay at home seemed much more self-confident when facing the often scary prospect of going to the dentist. Those children had much less separation anxiety. They had learned that their moms could be counted on to be there when they needed them and that their moms wouldn't steer them wrong. I made a mental note of that and it further reinforced my decision to be an at-home mom."

Former teachers commented similarly. Rebecca said, "Working in the school system allowed me to see first-hand the consequences that a mother's working has on her children." During her eleven years in the classroom, Mary Ann "saw many examples of children in day-care situations and the effects it had on them." From her observations, Mary Ann reached this conviction: "I feel very strongly that, if at all possible, mothers are to be at home." Another woman, who taught for seven years, said she noticed "behavioral differences between day-care children and home-based children." Her experience as a teacher influenced her decision to be at home with her own children.

As mentioned in chapter four, parents' decisions about a season at home are often influenced by their own childhood experiences. Rick Cole said that he and his wife "both agreed that during our childhoods we liked the fact that our mothers were at home, especially in the early school years. We decided that we wanted to give our child that same sense of security, that same sense of home."

One mother of three recalled: "I became a latchkey kid before the phrase was even invented. Summers were full days of being alone in the morning and spending every afternoon at the town pool where my mother dropped me off after lunch. We had one or two weeks a year to really be together." Not surprisingly, this woman's commitment to full-time mothering is very strong.

Sandra described her husband, Ben, as enthusiastic about the fact that she works part-time in order to maximize her time with their daughter. "He wants Bethany and me to be together," she said. "As a child he always came home to an empty home, and I still hear the sadness in him when he describes that feeling."

Mary Ann was also influenced by her childhood: "My mother was at home while I grew up. It was a secure feeling for me to have her there at all times. She was always available to be at special things going on at school and always willing to help at school parties and things, which made me feel proud. It definitely affects my views on being at home with my daughter. It was an example I wanted to follow."

Dee had similar recollections: "My mother was always there and able to participate in all our activities. It greatly affects my views about being at home. She planted the seeds for my desire to be at home."

Mary Bollinger, the only single mom in my sample, works at home full-time doing medical transcription. Her typical workday lasts ten to twelve hours, beginning in the wee hours before her son awakes and sometimes continuing after supper until she goes to bed. Her willingness to endure such a grueling schedule reflects her extraordinary commitment to being an at-home mom.

I asked Mary why she chose to work at home. Like other parents in my survey, Mary cited her childhood experience. Mary was a latchkey kid who felt "there was just something missing when I came home and Mom wasn't there." She remembers feeling "emptiness and just wanting my mother there." She vowed that her children would never come home to an empty house. Today, reported Mary, "My satisfaction from my work comes primarily from knowing I'm here for my son."

These parents illustrate an observation made by Charesa, an at-home mother of four: "We always fall back on the way we were brought up. When we feel good about our background, we rely on it even more."

How a Season at Home Benefits Our Kids

Strong Values and Character Qualities. Many parents in my survey felt that a mother at home had greater opportunities for shaping the values and morals of her children, instilling confidence, and teaching them to love God.

"We felt it extremely important," said Cami, thirty-three, "that we instill the love and affection, convictions and beliefs that we have, and not leave that responsibility to a stranger." Patti, who has a son and daughter, said that her being at home gives her children stability and "allows them to be taught my morals and values through day-to-day living by example."

Jan, thirty-three, exchanged a high-paying corporate job for part-time, at-home work in order to care for her children at home. "I've had teachers tell me they could tell I was a stay-at-home mother because my kids are much less aggressive, much more polite," she related. "They have confidence about them. You can tell they feel loved. I believe that the odds of them turning into healthy, God-fearing, God-serving adults are much greater with me at home than if I would have been in the corporate rat race."

Amy, thirty-one, had a strong sense of mission: "I want to play a key role in their character development and in teaching them values, responsibility, and love for the Lord. I wouldn't want to place my children in someone else's care because I feel God gave me the responsibility to raise them in a godly home."

Ron Kessinger, a thirty-nine-year-old father, told me that he feels being home with a full-time mom gives his daughter a sense of love. He observed, "It gives her a sense of stability, of confidence in who she is." Like Amy, he feels that teaching his daughter to love the Lord is a high priority, and one best served by having a season at home. "Whatever decision that child makes," he said, "is eternal."

Quality Care. A number of parents pointed out that by being their child's primary caretaker, they were assured of high quality care.

Twenty-eight-year-old Kris commented, "I don't ever have to worry about my child being hurt physically or emotionally. . . . And it's pretty tough to put a price tag on that!" Rebecca, the twenty-nine-year-old mother of a five-month-old, said, "The best part about being at home is knowing that I don't have to be concerned about someone else not caring for my daughter as I would wish."

"When my child has his first questions about God," said one young mother, "I want to be the one providing the answers, not some child care provider with whose background I am unfamiliar." Forty-three-year old Melanie has been an at-home mom since her oldest child was born. "Children's values, beliefs, personality, and morals are formed at an early age," she told me. "I don't want outsiders to spend more time with my children during these crucial years than I do."

Perhaps Michelle summed up the substitute-care issue when she observed, "No one will love your children like you do."

How a Season at Home Enhances Parenting

Narrowing the Channel Strengthens the Stream. Several parents said that allowing the mother to concentrate on one priority—parenting—instead of juggling the dual priorities of working and parenting, resulted in better mothering.

Rick Cole said that because his wife, Gail, is at home, his daughter, Jessica, "benefits from a mother who has the energy to help her with homework and to talk about the things that come up during her day." He explained, "I know that if Gail worked a full-time job outside the home she wouldn't have the same level of energy and the ability to focus her attention on Jessica."

Kris, who has worked in both banking and corporate sales, observed, "After working an eight-hour day, getting dinner on the table, and cleaning up, a child is not getting the whole mother, but what is left over." Kris has chosen a season at home, she says, because "I want to be able to give my son both quality and quantity time."

Kate, thirty-seven, is the mother of three children, ages eleven, nine, and two. Five-and-a-half years ago, she realized that exhaustion was sapping her effectiveness as a parent: "I was so tired when I got home from a full day's work to face a full evening's work of laundry, cooking, etc. It was hard to respond to my children and spend the quality time with them that I wanted to spend and felt they needed."

Things have changed for Kate since she started her season at home. "I can be here when my family needs me," she reported. "I think my children have a greater sense of love and security with me staying at home full-time."

Life in the Slow Lane Is a Plus. Several parents felt the quality of their parenting was enhanced by the flexibility and slower pace inherent to a season at home. "I spend time with each child individually when they need me to," Kelly, a thirty-five-year-old mother of three, said. "I can drop everything I am doing to spend time with them if they need it. I couldn't do that if I were working. I also don't have my mind on problems at work when I am with [my kids]."

One father ventured to suggest that when mom is at home, "the home is maintained better." He believes that kids benefit from a more organized, well-run household. When mothers are at home, he pointed out, "the beds tend to get made more regularly, the clothes tend to get ironed a little more regularly, that kind of thing." Mary Ann agreed: "I can get many things done during the day that I would need to do at night or on weekends if I worked. This allows more free, fun time for activities as a complete family." Beside that, she said, "I'm much less stressed out than if I were working outside the home."

A Full-time Parent Is an Asset to the Working Parent. I

asked psychologist Joe Verga whether having his wife, Heather, at home full-time with their three sons helped him be a better father. "Absolutely!" he responded. "She's very tuned in to the kids, much more than I can be because I have so much less time with them. And when we talk, she gives me insights about them and she can alert me to things that may need my attention, whether it may be more attention for one of the kids or a discipline problem or something they need to learn that I can teach them. It's a real sense of partnership; we're a team. Our goal is to give these kids the best possible start in life we can give them, and she's contributing a tremendous amount to my understanding about the children."

Ron Kessinger made a similar observation. Ron's wife, Judy, stays at home full-time with their three-year-old daughter, Sarah. "It gives me a benefit," he said. "Judy builds Daddy up in front of Sarah when I'm not around. Judy gets to tell her what Daddy is doing, where he's at, how Daddy feels about Sarah. She's kind of my advocate, in a way, building that relationship up for me."

How We Handle Criticism

As we noted, parents who choose a season at home are sometimes dealt unfair criticism. Staying at home for a season often means marching to a different drummer, in spite of the pressures and opinions of others. The choice to be at home requires that we take criticism in stride, while calmly continuing to pursue the goals that seem wise and sensible to us as we weigh our options before God.

Since moms often receive the bulk of the criticism, I asked mothers to tell me how they handle criticism about being at home. Most mothers, it seems, respond in one of two ways: they ignore the criticism or launch a verbal defense of their at-home status.

Paula takes the first approach: "I ignore it—to each his own." Shannon agreed: "I generally ignore criticism of my staying home and chalk it up to their ignorance of the situation." However she admitted, "I haven't always done this well, and there are times when I fight back with, 'How can bringing up tomorrow's leaders to be secure, sensitive, intelligent, loving humans be a waste of anyone's time?'"

Holly and Kris take a laid-back, good-natured approach. "I try not to take it personally,"said Holly. "I stick to my belief that it is a good use of my time." Kris agreed: "I'm proud of what I do and know that I'm spending my time making an eternal investment, and I think it shows. I'm on the offensive and not the defensive."

Kathie's attitude has mellowed with time and experience: "When my children were infants, I felt a greater need to defend my position that being at home made a difference. The older my children get, the more situations I handle where I know that my being there makes a tremendous difference, the less I feel a need to defend myself."

A woman's outward response is not always an indication of her inner feelings, however. While enduring or defending criticism, moms at home often feel angry or hurt. Cami and Mary Ann were honest about their feelings. "You can get overlooked in conversations with others who insinuate that you have no mind and have no intelligent life as we know it, just because you stay at home," Cami said. "Honestly, deep inside, I want to slap them and tell them how shallow and selfish their way of looking at life is. But I grit my teeth, smile, and tell them that this is the way my husband and I planned it: that we agreed that I would get my career under way and then put it on hold to stay at home and raise our children."

Mary Ann said, "Sometimes I'm crushed, sometimes I'm defensive, but I always come back to the thought that the way they see it compared to the way the Lord and my family see it—criticism is to be expected."

Although many of the women I surveyed had experienced criticism for being at home, none of them appeared to take it seriously. When a woman believes in what she's doing and is comfortable with her decision to be at home, criticism just doesn't stick. "I feel so worthwhile as a mother," explained Rebecca. "I know in my heart that I'm doing the right thing for myself and the future of my daughter."

The best defense against criticism is a good attitude! The next time you get some version of the "And what do *you* do?" question, why not look the naysayer in the eye and respond with something perky and enthusiastic? A heartfelt "I'm at home with my kids for a few years—and I *love* it!" tends to turn criticism into curiosity. And while you're having the fun of disarming critics with your positive attitude, listen to your own words. They will validate you and remind you of the importance of your at-home role.

PART
TWO

BUT HOW
CAN I?

SEVEN

Decisions

When I was debating about whether to work or not after our first child, I realized no one had ever said to me that they regretted staying at home with their kids. But I often heard, "I wish we had tried it with me staying home." That gave me courage to try.

—Wendy, thirty-four, mother of two

In her book *Sequencing*, Arlene Cardozo wrote that deciding "whether both partners will work full-time is almost always a values decision."[1] When first confronted with the task of making this decision, parents may not be sure what they want for themselves or what they think is best for their children. Gradually, through discussion, prayer, reading, and personal reflection, parents come to recognize their values: what really matters to them about work and parenting issues. There is, perhaps, no other major decision that more effectively reveals and clarifies for parents the values they hold most dear. Those values, more than anything else, determine the choices they will make regarding a season at home.

FOUR IMPORTANT VALUES

There are four values with special significance for decisions about work and parenting. The Bible offers perspectives applicable to all four.

The Value of Self

When Mary Howe left IBM to stay at home with her daughters, it was because, she says, "I knew in my heart that God was guiding me to go part-time or quit." When her company said "full time or no time," Mary said good-bye and began "one of the most difficult years of my life."

Mary's difficulty lay not in circumstances, but in how she saw herself. "I went from my whole self-esteem being wrapped up in 'I'm a marketing rep with IBM' to 'I'm a housewife.'" As a person, Mary had not changed. Only her job description had changed. But by making a choice she felt good about—staying at home—she found that she no longer felt good about herself. Many women who leave their jobs to come home share Mary's experience.

Since that first difficult year, something has changed inside Mary. Today she no longer suffers from low self-esteem. There is more to her story. Mary took action. She began with prayer. She sought out the fellowship of other mothers at home and found some former professionals like herself ("all kinds of intelligent women who had made the choice to stay home").

With prayer and the encouragement of new friends, Mary slowly realized that God was speaking to her. "God was telling me that what he thought of me was what was important, not what other people thought. And that I should take pride in the fact that I was doing what he wanted me to do and feel good about that."

Mary discovered that her worth and purpose lay, not in her job title, but in surrender to Christ. John 15:4 teaches the principle of *abiding*. Jesus said, "Abide in Me, and I in you. As the branch cannot bear fruit of itself, unless it abides in the vine, so neither can you, unless you abide in Me" (NASB).

112

The Greek word for abide is *meno*. It means "to lodge," "to dwell at one's own house," or "to be constantly present to help one."[2]

When we surrender ourselves to the will of God and rest in his care as serenely as a branch rests in a vine, something mysterious and wonderful begins to take place. As we *meno* in God, and he in us, our lives become an expression of this word. We become increasingly content to "dwell at [our] own house" and be "constantly present to help" our children.

In abiding, we discover not only the value of self, but the joy of being ourselves, irrespective of the work we do.

The Value of Money and Possessions

We live in a material world. We have material needs. The Bible teaches that God is not only aware of all of our needs, but that he willingly meets them (Matthew 6:8, 25–33; 7:7–11; Philippians 4:19). But it's easy to get material things and money out of focus. Jesus cautioned, "Watch out! Be on your guard against all kinds of greed; a man's life does not consist in the abundance of his possessions" (Luke 12:15). The best way to discern our present priorities is to study our checkbooks. Jesus said, "For where your treasure is, there your heart will be also" (Matthew 6:21).

Rick Cole commented on the lesson he learned about possessions: "From the perspective of having been a two-income family, from the perspective of having been a very aggressive ladder climber in the business world, and from the perspective of having a child with her mother at home, I've stumbled upon something that God has known all along, but that it took Rick thirty-something years to figure out. And it's this: Income is not the end-all and be-all of why we are here. Material things are not why we are alive."

The Value of People

Jesus said, "Greater love has no one than this, that he lay down his life for his friends" (John 15:13). Christ's death

113

on the cross is the ultimate indicator of our worth: he voluntarily laid down his life for us and he considers us his friends. So precious are we to him that Jesus said, "The very hairs of your head are all numbered" (Luke 12:7). Further, he is "intimately acquainted" with every detail of our lives (Psalm 139:3 NASB). In God's sight, people are supremely valuable—so valuable that Jesus said, "I chose you" (John 15:16). That's you, personally!

Sometimes we must make choices. In some cases, the only way to have a season at home is to choose between the people we call family and a larger income. This was the case for Kelly's family, who had the lowest income in my survey. But Kelly decided this: "What is more important to me than money and having things is good relationships with family members. Therefore, it is more important that I stay home with my children than that I get to eat out every week or get things."

The Value of Sacrificing for a Goal

Jesus said that the kingdom of heaven "is like a merchant looking for fine pearls. When he found one of great value, he went away and sold everything he had and bought it" (Matthew 13:45–46). This verse does *not* mean that being at home with your kids will be heaven on earth! It *does* illustrate, however, that sacrifice may be necessary in order to obtain something you regard as having great value, like a season at home.

Invariably, raising children involves some sacrifice. All parents sacrifice sleep, personal time, and personal desires in order to meet the needs of their children. The decision about having a parent at home full-time can be tough because it challenges parents to a new level of sacrifice.

Choosing a lesser standard of living is making a sacrifice. Choosing to set aside a career is a sacrifice. Choosing to spend endless hours with immature, demanding, needy people (children) instead of adults is also a sacrifice. Yet when those sacrifices are made willingly, as a reflection of personal convictions, or values, they are accompanied by joy and a sense of well-being.

Shannon expressed it like this: "The peace in my heart that comes from knowing I am doing what God has called me to do to the best of my abilities, the joy in knowing my children have had the best I could give them, the love I receive abundantly at unsuspecting moments—these are the best things about being at home. These are the things that make it worth the sacrifice!"

A JOINT DECISION

In two-parent families, the decision to have one parent at home full-time must be a joint decision. When parents have similar values, are willing to make similar sacrifices, and can agree on a strategy for implementing their goals, such decisions are relatively easy to make. Sherry, thirty-six, said that she and her husband "are in agreement on how we are raising our child. We both know that there have to be sacrifices made, and we're realistic in our expectations." Mary Ann said that deciding whether she should stay at home was easy because, "My husband and I felt exactly the same way about it."

Joe Verga told me that he and his wife, Heather, each grew up believing that they didn't have "to compete with other people or other standards of living." The Vergas share values that enable them to live happily on one income, and they have done so for all twenty-two years of their marriage, giving Heather the opportunity to be at home with their children. "We don't feel like we have to have a lot of stuff to be okay," said Joe. "We feel okay in Christ; we feel okay with each other; and we feel okay because we feel we're doing right by our kids."

But He Wants Me to Work!

A difference of opinion concerning a season at home may or may not reflect a difference in the basic values of each spouse. Whether it does or not, when a couple finds themselves unable to agree, it is time for them to talk. Open, honest discussion is the only way to gain an understanding of each other's point of view and to chart a unified course of action.

The three most important areas to discuss are *fears*, *feelings*, and *finances*. Suggested agendas for meaningful discussion in these areas can be found at the end of this chapter and the next. (Warning: Discussion may yield some surprises.)

Fears. Surprise number one for many couples is the discovery that what appeared to be a difference in values was, in fact, a manifestation of fear. Discussion about fears is important because men and women are likely to harbor different fears about life on one income. Fears can stem from the anticipated realities of a season at home, and also from the vibes we get from our culture and our peers. Because men and women may focus on different aspects of these same issues and messages, the potential for misunderstanding is great.

A woman may fear isolation, loneliness, and boredom. She may fear losing touch with her profession, thereby becoming less important. A man may fear the burden of becoming the sole provider for his family. He may also fear that as the children become a greater focus for his wife, he will become less important to her. Both may fear the pinch of living on less income or going into debt. Both may also fear criticism from co-workers or extended family.

The activity of talking through these fears, in and of itself, may be enough to resolve some of them or to spark a creative plan for avoiding problems.

Feelings. As has been previously noted, men and women generally process their work and parenting roles differently. Men attend to their duties sequentially: when they are at work, they work; when they are at home, they function as dad. Not so with working mothers. Emotionally, they operate in a dual capacity all the time. That's why leaving a baby or a child with a caretaker feels differently to a woman than it does to a man. Men, as a rule, have less difficulty dropping a child off at the sitter's and proceeding on with the day's business. A woman, more typically, feels that something is missing when she arrives at her office. And something *is* missing. It's her heart, and she left it back at the sitter's.

The difference between how it feels to be a mother and how it feels to be a father catches many couples by surprise. It can also cause problems. When a couple agrees that both spouses will continue to work while raising their children and make plans accordingly, things can go seriously awry if the mother suddenly changes her mind. A husband who thought there was a workable plan in place may even become angry when it seems that his wife wants to abandon the plan midstream. Tara and her husband, Brian, experienced this dilemma.

Tara explained, "I had always assumed I'd go back to work for financial reasons." But after the baby was born, Tara fell in love with her daughter in a way that caught her off guard. She realized that, more than anything, she wanted to stay at home with her baby. When their baby was six weeks old, Tara had to return to work as planned, but, she recalled, "I resented every minute." Meanwhile, she said, Brian "resented my wanting to be at home and expected me to help out financially." Tara was so miserable that Brian finally told her to quit her job. She did—and Brian panicked! Tara lamented, "I had to go back the next day and take back my resignation." It was more than two years later before this couple finally agreed upon a plan that allowed Tara to stay at home.

Unlike Brian, other husbands may be only temporarily dismayed by a proposed change in plans. If the wife's newfound desire to stay at home makes sense to him as well, he may easily agree to a revision in their course. Rebecca and her husband, Paul, are one couple who had little difficulty re-negotiating their plans.

Rebecca said, "I had always known that I would return to work shortly after I had my children." But during her pregnancy, Rebecca had a change of heart. The desire to stay at home became a growing conviction. She knew this would pose a significant problem. "Since my goal was to return to work," she explained, "my husband and I had not made plans financially" to accommodate a season at home. "At first," said Rebecca, "I was very hesitant to discuss this with Paul, due to the fact that we were counting on my income. . . . When I finally talked with him about it he was very supportive."

Working and staying at home are emotional issues, as much as they are practical matters. If a couple's discussion is to lead them to a greater understanding of each other and to a mutually acceptable course of action, feelings need to be recognized as a legitimate aspect of their discussion.

Fruitful discussion has two equal parts: talking and listening. Each partner needs the opportunity to express how he or she feels about the issues, and each partner needs to listen attentively in order to comprehend the emotions behind the spouse's words. The goal is mutual understanding.

When one partner feels far more strongly about his or her position than the other partner, psychologist Joe Verga suggested they rely on a biblical principle: "I think this gets into the whole issue of how you view submitting to one another. We're called to submit to one another in love. I think, in a way, we may be ignoring the voice of God when we ignore a strong conviction that our spouse has." One way to test the waters, suggested Dr. Verga, is to attempt a particular course of action on a trial basis.

What if both partners have equally strong, opposing views? Rick Cole suggested that the answer to such an impasse is compromise: "He may have a financial goal in mind. She may have a family goal in mind. Do these goals have to be mutually exclusive? Probably not." The couple should clarify their individual goals, he explained and "seek ways in which they are both attainable. . . . All of life is a negotiation. And the win-win concept of negotiation makes people a lot happier and solves more problems than the win-lose philosophy."

Finances. The most common obstacle to a season at home is family finances. Perhaps stated more accurately, it is a husband and wife's perception of their finances and the importance they attach to a particular standard of living which allows them to feel they can or cannot afford a season at home. I make this important distinction on the basis of the things parents shared with me on surveys and in personal interviews.

Every mother or father in my sample represented a family currently in a season at home, yet their incomes ran the gamut. At one end of the scale were women like Charesa and Kate, whose family incomes were somewhere in excess of $100,000 a year. Both women acknowledge their enviable financial position with gratitude to God. Kate said, "The Lord has truly blessed us in many ways." Thanks to her husband's lucrative job, Karen admitted that she has been able "to stay at home with few sacrifices."

At the opposite end of the scale were families like April's. April and her husband, Bob, were committed to having a season at home, despite financial hardship. April explained: "I stayed home with my children for seven years, until they were in school, and my husband only made $12,000 in yearly salary. They were good years that I'll never forget, but they were hard years. We never went hungry; God always provided for our needs, although not many of our wants at the time." Today April's family of four has a larger income (between $25,000 and $35,000), about half of which April earns by working part-time as a housekeeper.

When I interviewed Rick Cole, he had been without a full-time job for fifteen months. "I guess the most accurate way to describe me is under-employed," he said. "I do have some things that I'm working on with a local non-profit organization; I am earning some income, but it's not full-time. It's not what I've trained for or done in the past." In spite of having a dramatically reduced income for an extended period, the Coles have managed to keep their at-home season intact: Rick's wife, Gail, is still at home full-time.

Given his employment status, I was curious about how Rick would answer a question I had asked the other fathers: Do you ever feel anxious or worried about being the sole financial support of your family? Like the other dads, Rick responded in the affirmative: "Of course!" He explained: "Even when I had no reason to think my job was in jeopardy, there was always a level of concern. However, I must say that God has taught me not to be a worrier about it. Plan the best you can, be prudent, but then recognize that it's all in God's hands anyway. Looking back over the past fifteen months, I haven't had a full-time job this whole time, and God has provided for us every step of the way. So why should I start worrying now?"

The Bottom Line. The other families in my sample had incomes that fell somewhere between the two extremes just cited. For this majority of families, an average, middle-class income was adequate for their season at home, making it neither a bitter sacrifice nor a walk on easy street. As I perused the wide range of family incomes and comments I gleaned from my surveys and interviews, it became clear that the deciding factor for these season-at-home families was not finances. It was desire. The common denominator among these families was simply this: they *wanted* a season at home.

The most important question for most couples to negotiate is not, Can we afford a season at home? The critical question is, How badly do we want to do this?

Mary Howe has observed that when couples (for whatever reason) really don't want a season at home, mothers often sing a common refrain: "I have to work." Mary, whose former income contributed $50,000 a year to the family budget, knows the "have to work" lyric well; it used to be her song. But Mary has changed her tune: "Yes, you have to work to have a nice, big home and new cars and all the luxuries. But you don't *have* to work."

Certainly there are extraordinary circumstances that *require* a dual income every step of the way. But apart from those exceptions, why do so many parents feel they both "have to work" full-time when their children are young?

Ultimately, most people do those things in life that they *want* to do. And many mothers with young children often *want* to work for two common reasons.

Why Moms "Have to" Work. Parents quite naturally want to provide their children with the best they possibly can—the best toys, the best clothes, and the best early learning experiences. It feels good to dress a cherubic little child in clothing that says B'Gosh or Polo. It also feels good to put name-brand toys under the Christmas tree or around the birthday cake. To many of us, those tangible commodities are evidence that we are good parents and that we love our kids.

Certainly name-brand clothes and the hot TV commercial toys will eventually matter to most kids. But during the red-light years, especially, clothing labels and brand-name toys are virtually meaningless to a child. Very young children are oblivious to whether their clothing was purchased at a yard sale or a department store. They are as content with cousin Tom's hand-me-down toys as they are with those sporting a famous logo.

The truth is that owning name-brand clothing, toys, and baby equipment meets an emotional need for parents, not for the child. Young children's greatest needs are not met by things that can be purchased for them. And when both parents work full-time in order to provide their young children with "the best," they make a serious mistake.

The second reason many moms bypass a season at home is that a job often meets an emotional need common to women. Women, far more than men, thrive on interpersonal relationships, companionship, and emotional nurture. Women need friendships and a social support system.

In many neighborhoods, the only woman at home during the day is the courageous and lonely mother of preschoolers. The office, the lab, the classroom, and the factory have become the neighborhoods of the nineties. Many women go to work simply because they are lonely and want to surround themselves with people.

The good news is that both of the "have to work"

concerns are easily resolved. Information about the developmental needs of children can redefine what it means for parents to give their children the best. A stay-at-home mother's emotional and social needs can be abundantly met as she begins to meet and network with other moms in the same profession.

Thus, with a combination of factual information, creativity, and common sense, the have-to-work philosophy quickly dies a natural death. When parents are convinced about the importance of a season at home, they will search diligently to find a way to make such a season financially feasible, with God's help.

Before we go any further into the nitty gritty of dollars and cents, two important questions must be answered: First, are you convinced of the wisdom and benefits of a season at home? And second, do you really want a season at home? If you are unsure about your answer to either or both of these questions, you will profit greatly by discussing these issues with your spouse. If your answers to both questions are yes, your chances for success are excellent. You have already crossed the first major hurdle!

While finances are important, there are a few other issues you will want to include in your decision-making discussions with your spouse.

The Down Side

A season at home is a wonderful thing, but it is also a difficult undertaking for reasons which may not be readily apparent to those in the throes of making a decision. In the interest of providing a reality check for decision-makers, I asked mothers to tell me what, for them, was the hardest part of being at home. Here are some representative comments:

"In the first year at home, it was exhaustion," Sherry recalled. "It was more of a mental exhaustion due to the amount of attention that a newborn and a toddler require.

Now, it's more a struggle with boredom—the same old routine."

"It's hard to find breaks," Charesa confided. "It's also hard to have a devotional time. The house gets messed up easier. It's harder to be on a schedule, too."

"One of the hardest things is the lack of perks," admitted Lisa. "At work, there are paychecks, evaluations, and the feeling of a job well done. At home, everything you do gets undone just as quickly as it gets done."

Karen added, "For me, the hardest part is not having adult companionship during the day."

Shannon cited a variety of factors: "Lack of cash. The seclusion. I also struggle with exhaustion. The twelve- to fourteen-hour shift, seven days a week does tend to wear me down on occasion."

"I get lonely at times," Melanie said. "I also stay tired. Being an older mother (age forty-three with preschool children), I don't have the energy of a younger woman."

"I struggle with feeling inadequate to provide enough stimulation and meet all the demands of my child and feeling overwhelmed by all that I need to get done, knowing I need to just forget it and spend time with my child," explained Holly. "I struggle with slight depression at times and with fatigue a lot."

Staying at home is hard work! One survey of at-home moms revealed that 42 percent work fourteen or more hours a day caring for their children.[3] The energy drain that naturally results from these long workdays can sometimes be mystifying to husbands. Lisa, who experiences exhaustion parenting her three children, told me, "Most of the time, my husband expresses understanding. But I know that his real understanding is very limited: he is not here day after day." Said Holly, "It is hard for my husband when I'm so exhausted at the end of the day that I don't feel up to spending time with him."

Exhaustion and the other day-to-day realities of full-time mothering must be squarely faced, along with the changes that may be introduced into the marriage relationship. Cami said she would remind a mother who was considering a season at home that "if she thinks she's coming home to relax and play—forget it! Staying home with your children is a very selfless thing to do."

The Up Side

On a more positive note, it should be pointed out that the exhaustion-factor decreases dramatically as children get older. When my son was first born, a friend warned me that the first three years were the hardest. As a new mother, the thought of enduring sleep deprivation and exhaustion for three years sounded nightmarish! As it turned out, the first three years were indeed physically taxing, but looking back, they were also some of the sweetest years of my life.

Exhaustion aside, having the wife at home is usually a plus for the marriage. Arlene Cardozo noted, "Less stress on the marriage is a definite joint gain of sequencing."[4] Rick Cole offered this sentiment: "I think in every man there is still a little boy. And even though Gail is my spouse, to that little boy, it is nice to know that there is a mother in the home. Not *my* mother, but *a* mother. For me, it creates that certainty in my heart and in my mind, as I'm going about my business, that at the end of the day someone is going to be there, eager to see me. When I get home I won't have to think, Oh, I don't get to see her tonight because she's off at a board meeting."

One More Decision

Any couple weighing the merits of a season at home should include a discussion of housework. Like every other aspect of sequencing, there is no one-size-fits-all way to take care of this constant duty. Some families hire help. Some parents share the load more or less equally. Some families assign all duties to the wife because she is at home and they consider housework part of her job. What seems most workable to you? What's fair, given your circumstances? Whose job is housework? These are matters for discussion.

When I surveyed mothers at home I asked them how housework was accomplished in their families. Here's what they told me.

Hiring Help. Only four of the thirty women have regular, paid help to assist with the housework. Not surprisingly, these were women with substantial family incomes. Three of the four indicated that their household income was $85,000 a year or more; the fourth said her family income was between $55,000 and $65,000. A fifth woman, Pam, said, "I had paid help when the children were infants."

Sharing the Load. Eight women said that their husbands helped with housework. Carol, the mother of two boys, said, "My husband helps me daily—he gets paid with love!" Three others indicated that their spouses helped on a regular basis. Four said that their husband helped out occasionally. Three women had occasional help from their older children.

Part of Mom's Job. Sixteen women said that they had no help with the housework. They expressed a variety of sentiments about having to do it all. Holly sounded weary: "Because I'm a full-time homemaker, I feel pressured to take care of the majority of the household management because my husband's job is so demanding. I often feel overwhelmed at all I have to do." Wendy injected a bit of humor: "Help with the housework! In my dreams! I heard (on the Focus on the Family radio program), 'a house should be clean enough to be healthy and cluttered enough to be happy.' We're real happy!"

My personal vote goes to the share-the-work economy plan: no hired help, but an equitable sharing of the load between spouses and, according to age and ability, among the children as well. This is the most practical solution for those couples who can't (or don't want to) hire help. While this sounds good on paper, unless *both* spouses sincerely share this view and unless the husband actually has the time to help, housework either goes undone or falls to the wife. This is unfortunate, because mothers at home typically work more hours a day and, in many ways, work harder, than many mothers employed outside the home.

The mom-does-it-all approach to housekeeping is unfortunate, too, because it overburdens mothers compared to other family members, often to the point of exhaustion. This models imbalance and perhaps even martyrdom for the children (not traits most of us want to pass to the next generation). The ideal scenario has both parents and each child, to the extent they are capable, functioning as a team to shoulder equitable portions of household responsibility.

When dad is too busy and the children are too young to help, instead of over-taxing the mother, if at all possible, the family should employ paid help. This need not be a budget buster. Many teenagers, for example, do adult-quality work for less money per hour than it would cost to hire a housecleaning service.

One couple solved their standoff about housework after the wife read the children's story *The Little Red Hen* aloud to her husband. Her experience had been a real-life version of this tale: Who will help me wash the casserole dish? Who will help me pick up the toys? Who will help me fold the laundry? The discussion that followed the reading session permanently changed this couple's approach to household chores.[5] (This story appeared in *Guideposts* magazine, and I loved it!)

DECISIONS

The important decisions about work and parenting should be made only after significant discussion has taken place between husband and wife. For Christians, earnest prayer is essential as well. The following is suggested as a springboard to a discussion about feelings, fears, and housework. A similar agenda for discussing finances appears at the end of the next chapter. Together, these agendas can aid in decision making.

Preparation for Discussion

For a period of thirty days (or whatever amount of time works best), both husband and wife agree to pray individually about the decisions they must make as a couple. During this one-month period, each of them will keep a daily journal of their prayers, feelings, and concerns. They will not discuss the progression of their thinking with their partner.

At the end of the thirty-day period, they will spend an extended time together sharing excerpts from their journals and explaining how they believe God has led them individually. This method assures that both husband and wife will have taken adequate time to assess their individual values and goals and will have given God an opportunity to impress their thinking.

The couple then discusses their individual answers to the following questions and examine areas where they agree and disagree with each other.

Agenda for Discussion

I. Feelings
   A. Personal Background
      1. Did your mother work or stay at home when you were growing up?
      2. What are your memories, positive or negative, about her working or staying at home?
      3. When you were a child, how did you feel about her working or staying at home?
      4. Looking back, how do you feel about it now?
      5. What, if anything, do you wish had been different?
   B. Present Feelings
      1. As you look back over your journal entries, what emerge as your strongest convictions?
      2. Rank these statements on a scale of one to ten (ten being most important):
         a. I want a good standard of living for my family.

b. I want my children's daily care to be provided by a parent.

c. My (or my spouse's) career is important to me (her).

3. How do you think having had a working mother or an at-home mother influences what you would like for your own children?

4. If at least one spouse is not presently working: How do you think you would feel about leaving your children with a caretaker?

5. If both spouses are presently working: What feelings do you experience when leaving your children with their caretaker?

6. If you could change anything about your present child-care arrangement what would it be? Why?

7. For wife, if working: If you were to quit your job, what would you miss about working?

8. For wife: What appeals to you about a season at home?

9. For husband: What appeals to you about having your wife work? What do you dislike?

10. For husband: What appeals to you about having your wife stay at home with the children? What do you dislike?

12. How do you think a season at home will affect your marriage?

13. Disregarding finances, rank this statement using the 1–10 scale: I want a season at home for our family.

II. Fears

A. For women: Which of these is a concern to you when you think about staying at home with your children? Number your top three concerns.

_____ becoming isolated or out of touch with friends

_____ getting bored

_____ losing job-related self-esteem

_____ not having enough money

_____ going into debt

_____ lack of confidence about parenting skills

_____ being unsure about whether I really want to be at home

_____ exhaustion and stress

_____ criticism from others

_____ negative effect on marriage

_____ losing touch with my profession and not being able to land a good job later

_____ other (define)

_____ I'm uncomfortable, but not sure why

B. For men: Which of these is a concern to you when you think about your wife staying at home with the children? Number your top three concerns.

_____ being the sole financial provider

_____ not having enough money

_____ going into debt

_____ having my wife be too tired to spend time with me

_____ becoming less important to my wife

_____ criticism from others

_____ negative effect on marriage

_____ wife losing touch with her profession and not being able to land a good job later

_____ being unsure about a season at home

_____ having more household responsibilities

_____ other (define)

_____ I'm uncomfortable, but not sure why

C. For both spouses:

1. Share your top three concerns with your spouse and tell why they are concerns for you.

2. What, to you, is the worst thing that could happen in the area of your primary concern?

3. What steps can the two of you take to prevent this from happening?

    4. What would you do to cope if it happened anyway?

    5. Repeat questions two through four in regard to your second and third greatest concerns.

III. Housework

  A. When you were growing up, how was housework handled in your family? (What contribution did each parent make? Did the children do housework?)

  B. Looking back, does this seem fair to you?

  C. How important is it to you to have an orderly, clean house? Compare your answer with your spouse's answer and discuss the implications.

  D. Ideally, how would you like to handle household chores: hire help, share the work, consider it part of the job of being at home full-time, or a combination of these approaches?

  E. If you choose a season at home, would this approach be practical? Would it be fair? If not, what do you think a fair and realistic approach would be?

  F. Do you think your children should help with the housework? Do you think they should be paid for doing chores?

As you complete your conversation, discuss what you think of this statement from Tara, a thirty-five-year-old mother of three: "Quitting work was not a tough decision—just a tough step."

EIGHT

Mission Impossible?
(Maybe Not!)

*The value of a sentiment is the amount of
sacrifice you are prepared to make for it.*
—John Galsworthy

For Amy, it started with a dream. She wanted "to raise a large family and buy a house without two full-time incomes." Many families view this as an impossible dream. But, said Amy, "I had a crazy notion that I could have both without the two-income/day-care frenzy that has become the norm for the modern American family." She set out to prove that it could be done.

Did she reach her goal? Judge for yourself.

Amy is a stay-at-home mom. Her husband, Jim, is a naval officer who earns $30,000 a year. While living on Jim's salary alone, in less than seven years Amy and Jim managed to save $49,000 in cash. During that same period of time, they also purchased $38,000 worth of appliances, furniture, and vehicles. What's more, they managed these impressive accomplishments while remaining debt free.

Today, Amy and Jim live in their dream house—a large, pre-1900 New England farmhouse with an attached barn. They are still debt free and Amy is at home full-time—with their *six* children.[1]

Amy Dacyczyn has proven that having a family and owning a home does not require two incomes. Her remarkable story has been told repeatedly by the national media. She's been a guest on *To Tell the Truth* and *Donahue*. *Parade* magazine did a cover story on the Dacyczyns, and they've been featured in *Yankee* magazine as well. In response to all this publicity, subscriptions to Amy's newsletter, *The Tightwad Gazette*, have poured in. She now mails out over 100,000 copies a month. Her new book by the same name is available in bookstores nationwide.

Amy's ideas have struck a nerve with the American public. But the notion that one can actually achieve the American dream by *saving* more instead of *earning* more is not a new idea. It's an old-fashioned value—thrift—whose time has come again.

The obvious payoffs of a frugal lifestyle, as exemplified by the Dacyczyns, are very appealing to many people, especially two-career couples who are tired of the corporate rat race and working mothers who are tired of daily separations from their children. More and more couples are beginning to realize that they, too, can realize their dreams—including the dream to have a season at home—by following in the Dacyczyns' footsteps.

But why am I telling you all this? Because you can do it, too!

FINANCES: PLANNING A STRATEGY

When a husband and wife decide that they want a season at home and that they are willing to do whatever it takes to make that happen, they can succeed in meeting that goal, but it won't happen by accident. A season at home often requires careful preparation. Couples need to develop a practical, realistic plan.

With a well-thought-out road map to chart the path to their goal, couples can make the wisest use of their available resources. Having a strategy can make a big difference, especially when finances are limited. As Robert Louis Stevenson is credited with having said, "Life is not a matter of holding good cards, but of playing a poor hand well."

I'd like to suggest a five-step financial approach to the goal of having a season at home. These five steps will help you play your financial hand to the best of your ability, helping you to work smarter (rather than harder), as you advance toward your goal. The steps are: tithe; plan ahead; assess current spending; economize; and if necessary, work at home.

The first four steps are covered in this chapter. The next chapter is devoted to step five, working at home.

STEP ONE: TITHE

You may or may not be tithing now. Maybe you've never heard of tithing. Tithing means giving a tenth of our income back to God. If you are already on a tight budget, tithing may sound like a dumb idea. Trust me—it's not! It's more like dropping a few seeds into the ground and getting an entire crop in return.

Tithing is a biblical concept, but it is found in ancient Greek history as well. After a military victory, the Greeks would gather up all their spoils in a heap. The very best spoils were placed in the top tenth of the heap and presented to their gods.[2] When we tithe, we give God the top tenth of our heap, so to speak.

In Mosaic law, God instructed the Jews to tithe from all their produce, flocks, and cattle. These tithes were given to the Levitical priests for their support. They, in turn, gave a tithe to support the high priest. In the New Testament, Jesus condemned the Pharisees' legalism in tithing, but affirmed that tithing was something they should have done (Matthew 23:23).

According to *Unger's Bible Dictionary*, tithing "constituted a practical confession and acknowledgment that the whole land, that all possessions in general, belonged to [God], and that it was he alone who conferred them upon those who enjoyed them."[3] Today we tithe for the same reason. We are telling God that we have not forgotten that he alone is the source of both our material and financial blessings.

At the human level, tithing is a good way to gauge our trust in God. When we reach the point of trusting him with our money, we can be sure we are trusting him to provide for us. Rick Cole explained it this way: "Until I gave my finances to God, I didn't really give him all of myself. And that, I think, for many men is a real stumbling block. They just can't seem to turn loose of their money." So how does this relate to a season at home? Rick said, "If we're going to hold back something and not put it in obedience to God by giving to his work, I really don't think we can expect his full blessing."

To financially survive a season at home, we need God's full blessing. Tithing is the one area where God challenges us to test him. Ponder Malachi 3:10: " 'Bring the whole tithe into the storehouse, that there may be food in my house. Test me in this,' says the Lord Almighty, 'and see if I will not throw open the floodgates of heaven and pour out so much blessing that you will not have room enough for it.' "

Does God keep his promises? Start tithing and see what happens!

STEP TWO: PLAN AHEAD

As evidenced by Tara and Rebecca's stories in the previous chapter, planning ahead for a season at home is not always possible. If you are at a point in life where planning ahead is still possible, this step is for you. By taking prudent action now, you can make it easier to stay at home later. If you are beyond the point where planning is possible, move on to step three.

For those in a position to plan, here are four important areas to address.

Debt. Debt can steal the opportunity to have a season at home. Proverbs 22:7 says that "the borrower becomes the lender's slave" (NASB). This is all too true when parents miss out on a season at home because they both have to work to repay their debts.

A season at home can be undertaken in spite of indebtedness, but it may be robbed of its joy because of it. Two of the couples in my survey were laboring under serious debt. "I don't think we have been very wise in some of our financial decisions," Holly admitted. "We now have $40,000 in loans to pay back and I feel very uncomfortable with that. I wish we had tightened our belts a bit more and not bought the size house we did." Kelly told a similar tale: "We are at present trying to get out of debt. This is why my husband has not finished college. However, the debt is not due to me not working. It is due to a lack of discipline in the use of credit cards."

Are you headed for trouble with indebtedness? Consumer Credit Counseling Service suggests these five danger signals:

1. Do you pay only the minimum on your monthly credit cards?
2. Do you use a credit card for groceries or other necessities?
3. Do you use credit to repay other debts? (That is, do you take out an advance on one card to pay off another?)
4. Is more than 20 percent of your monthly take-home pay used to pay consumer debt?
5. Are you unsure of how much you owe?

If you answered yes to more than one question, you may be on shaky financial ground.[4]

Are you anticipating a season at home? Now is the best time to reduce or eliminate debt. If you need help accomplishing this, contact your local Consumer Credit Counseling

Service or call the national hotline at 1-800-388-2227 to find the office nearest you. This quality counseling is provided free of charge to you, the consumer.

"If you live within your means," Joe Verga affirmed, "things work out." As we move toward becoming debt-free, God is honored and we gain new power to both establish and enjoy a season at home.

Savings. In sharp contrast to the parents battling debt, those who had had the foresight to save up for a season at home felt good about their preparation. Dee told me, "We actually saved my income for eight years so we could buy a house when the children came." Said Sherry, "We waited five years before having a baby, partly to make sure we could afford financially for me to stay home."

Rick Cole pointed out that saving is a smart thing to do, no matter what: "Even if you plan on having children and you don't plan on the mother staying at home, you never know when a layoff is coming; you never know when an illness is coming that's going to make you a one-income family anyway. So, it's wise to do the best you can *when* you can." Some financial planners recommend that a couple save until they accumulate the equivalent of three months' salary in their account. This money would provide a financial cushion in the event of a layoff, illness, or other emergency.

The biblical role model for saving is the ant. Proverbs 30:24–25 says that while ants are small, they are "extremely wise" because they plan ahead while they have the opportunity to do so. Ants "store up their food in the summer" before winter's chill sets in.

Using ants—and the Dacyczyns—as examples, families can build up their savings before winter (the at-home season) arrives. Two-income families, with their potential for saving one spouse's entire paycheck, may have a longer summer and be able to save up more money.

Think of the possibilities! If you managed to save as much as the Dacyczyns did ($49,000 in less than seven years), you could make a down payment on a house and invest or save the rest. If you already own a home, you could pay yourself a salary of $1,000 a month for four years—all of the red-light phase and part of the yellow.

Live on one income as soon as possible. Dee suggested that newlyweds "begin to prepare to stay home the first day of their marriage." Ron Kessinger asserted that the best way to do this is to "establish a lifestyle as if they only had one income." Ron, Dee, and other parents who have been there suggest that dual-income couples should start placing that extra paycheck in the bank as soon as possible so that the money can build up for insurance against emergencies, vacation funds, or major purchases.

When determining which check to put in the bank and which to live on, keep in mind that the at-home parent could be the father. Dual-income couples must determine which parent will work and which parent will stay at home. If the mother's job is more lucrative and if the father prefers to be the at-home parent, it may make more sense to plan for this arrangement from the outset.

Dee said young couples must set priorities. Ron agreed, and added: "When you have two incomes and you spend as though you have two incomes, when a child comes you may find it hard to stop. I think it's very crucial that you establish a pattern early on that is consistent with the priorities in your life."

Investigate work-at-home opportunities. If you think you may need to earn money by working at home, begin to investigate those opportunities *before* you quit working. Talk with your present employer about the possibility of working from home in the future. Telecommuting or freelancing may be realistic options in some cases. Part-time work or job sharing may be possibilities as well.

While you are still employed, make the most of the information and resources at your fingertips. Make in-house phone calls and utilize your network in other ways to investigate possibilities and make contacts that will come in handy later. Make plans to stay in touch with co-workers after you quit.

A SEASON AT HOME

STEP THREE: ASSESS CURRENT SPENDING

Here's how to assess your current spending and set the stage for economizing.

1. Keep a two-month spending log. For a period of sixty days, keep track of everything you spend. Each spouse should carry a notebook and record *every* expenditure, whether it is small (gum, stamps, nail polish, etc.) or large (house payment, car repair, etc.). Spend what you would normally spend; don't do anything differently because you are recording your purchases. At the end of two months you will have a good idea of where your money goes. You will also have a factual basis for determining any changes that would be needed if you decide on a season at home.

Keeping a spending log may seem like a hassle—and it is. But don't underestimate the importance of this step. The information you will gain is critical to succeeding at your goal of staying at home.

2. Identify all work-related costs. Some expenses are automatically eliminated when only one parent works outside the home. Many couples are surprised to discover how much it costs to work.

When Mary Ann and her husband first discussed the possibility of her staying at home, they were worried. "We wondered," she said, "how we could give up the income." Then they realized how much they had to spend in order for Mary Ann to bring home her paycheck. She ticked off a list of considerations: "When I worked, I spent much more on clothes. It costs to drive to work and back. Because of my working, we ate out three or four times a week. Because of two incomes, we did a lot more impulse buying."

According to a *Wall Street Journal* report, "two-earner families lose up to two-thirds of the second paycheck to work-related costs."[5] Child care alone often takes up to 10 percent of a couple's combined income.[6] Add to this expense the cost of lunches, taxes and social security, timesaving services such as housecleaning or lawn care, and at-home convenience foods, and it quickly becomes evident that unless a mother's paycheck is substantial, it may actually make more financial sense for her *not* to work. In their book *Staying Home: From Full-Time Professional to Full-Time Parent*, authors Darcie Sanders and Martha Bullen offer an important guideline. "One rule of thumb," they say, "is that you need to make roughly two and a half times your child-care costs for working outside the home to be economically advantageous."[7]

Amy Dacyczyn calculates that when work-related expenses are coupled with the higher tax bracket of combined incomes, a $15,000 annual salary can yield less than $4,000 in net income.[8] What parents have to decide is whether missing out on a season at home is worth $4,000 (or whatever their actual figure would be). Mary Ann and her husband concluded that as a two-income family, they "wouldn't gain much at all financially, but would sacrifice much emotionally." Mary Ann has been at home for the last three years.

When your two-month log is complete, identify every work-related expenditure—and subtract it from your budget.

STEP FOUR: ECONOMIZE

Wait until your sixty-day spending record is complete before you take this step. Each family must analyze its spending patterns and determine which of its expenses are essential and which are optional. How much you'll need to modify your present spending depends on the size of the gap between your income and your living expenses. Some families will need to make only minor adjustments. Others must make major changes in their lifestyles.

Executed properly, this step may eliminate the need for step five (working at home). Much depends on you. How resourceful are you? How practiced are you at delaying gratification? How much would you be willing to sacrifice in order to stay at home with your children? The way you answer these questions might make the impossible possible.

To begin economizing, go over your two-month log,

entry by entry. First, determine every essential, or necessary, expense. For example, food, the power bill, and gasoline would be necessary expenses. Think in terms of general categories (food, utilities, clothing, etc.) and note everything that relates to them. Don't confuse your task by editing out your doughnut purchase or the premium gas you bought by mistake. Be true to the record as it stands.

Color-code this essentials category of log entries with a Hi-Liter. Consider everything else in your log optional. Calling these expenditures optional doesn't mean you can do away with them wholesale or that you should. It simply distinguishes between those things essential for survival and other expenses.

Reduce Essential Expenses

Now it's time to wield the ax! Even though the entries you highlighted are necessary expenditures, there may be ways to decrease the amount you spend on essential goods and services. For example:

Food:

Eliminate junk food and soda.
Buy in bulk quantities.
Avoid prepackaged convenience food.
Eat out less often.
Make it yourself for less. (Compare the cost of a homemade pizza, for example, to the cost of having one delivered.)
Shop! Compare prices at different stores. Shop sales and at reduced-price places such as bakery outlets.
Grow a garden and can your own food.
Buy store brands.

Clothing:

Sew.
Shop at thrift shops, outlets, and end-of-season sales.
Check yard sales for children's clothing.

Auto:

Pump your gas. (Does it have to be the most expensive grade?)

Change your oil.

Rotate your tires.

Shop for the best insurance rates.

Utilities:

Be diligent about turning off lights, appliances, and televisions when not in use.

Wash clothes in cold water.

Hang wet clothes instead of running the dryer.

Lower the thermostat setting.

Write letters instead of calling long distance (29 cents versus multiple dollars).

This is by no means an exhaustive list of ways to reduce the cost of necessary expenditures. Brainstorm with your spouse about what you can do to reduce your basic cost of living. You might want to borrow some books from the library on this topic.

Reduce Optional Expenses

Now take a look at the items in your log which are not highlighted. Since these are not essential to survival, you will probably be able to save even more money by reducing or eliminating goods and services in this category.

Trim the Fat First. Look at what you waste or don't fully utilize. These are usually the most painless reductions you can make. Here are a few examples:

If you don't have time to read the newspaper every day, why not downgrade to a weekend subscription?

If you carry three premium cable channels, give up one or two to lower your bill. (Or cancel all three. Radical notion: might you be able to survive without cable TV?)

Cancel subscriptions to magazines you don't read or need.

Cancel record-of-the month, book-of-the month, and other of-the-month memberships.

If you didn't renew your health club membership, could you work out at home?

Does your dog need name-brand food?

Sacrifice Creatively

Once you've cut and reduced in all the relatively painless ways you can think of, it's time to take a serious look at the areas that may require bona fide sacrifice.

Sacrifice was a familiar word to many of the moms I surveyed. Shannon asked, rhetorically: "What do we sacrifice for me to stay home? Haircuts at the salon. New cars. A bigger home. HBO. Store-bought clothes. Trips to Disney. Eating out. Week-long vacations. Name-brand products. Long distance calls. Manicures. Facials. We have no charge cards—all purchases are with cash."

Carol gave a different list: "We have sacrificed new furniture, new curtains, new appliances, and new clothes and shoes. I've sacrificed good skin care products, jewelry, new pocketbooks, and wallets—I've carried the same worn-out wallet for twelve years! We've sacrificed hobbies with expensive accessories, like long-distance biking. We have never had a new car. Until recently—after twelve years of marriage and two children—we've never owned our own home. We've rented all these years."

Like Shannon and Carol, you may have to sacrifice something (or many things) in order to stay at home with your children. But before you fully embrace a lifestyle of sacrifice and deprivation, it may be helpful to gain some perspective by examining the meaning of *thrift*.

Year ago, some anonymous Yankee poet penned these immortal words:

Mission Impossible? (Maybe Not!)

Use it up, wear it out;
Make it do, or do without.

Is that an accurate definition of thrift? Is that what we're talking about here? Sort of, but not quite. Amy Dacyczyn described thrift (tightwaddery) this way: "Tightwaddery without creativity is deprivation. When there is a lack of resourcefulness, inventiveness, and innovation, thrift means doing without." But—and this is the key concept— "When creativity combines with thrift you may be doing without money, but you are not doing without."[9]

Here is what I think she means:

Creative thrift means that rather than do without, we learn a new skill. For instance, could you learn to groom your own poodle? Or cut your kids' hair? How about canning your own fruits and vegetables? What about painting your own house? Or steam cleaning your carpets? Or perming your own hair?

Creative thrift means that rather than do without, we do some things differently. Can you car pool to work? Pack your lunch? Borrow books, tapes, and videos from the library instead of buying them?

You can even learn to have fun in a different way. Instead of going out once a month with another couple for dinner and a movie, why not cook dinner at your house and rent a video? If you normally spend two weeks at the beach in the summer, how much could you save by going after Labor Day? (It's still plenty hot, but the beaches are less crowded and the motel rates are considerably lower.)

Creative thrift means that rather than do without, we regard resources with a new mindset. Frugal theory, so to speak, dictates that most commodities should be scrutinized with a view to possible re-use. Re-using or conserving resources is always more prudent than purchasing new ones.

The *Tightwad* book and newsletters are must reading for anyone enmeshed in the fast-food, throwaway mindset of American culture. The January 1993 newsletter included, among other things, advice on what to do with old egg cartons, room deodorizers, and used pregnancy test kits. The book by the same name contains a wealth of what-to-do-with information: crayon bits, milk jug rings, mesh onion bags, dryer lint, and half-eaten apples can be put to good use. Moth-eaten sweaters can be turned into mittens. Roll-on deodorant bottles can become paint applicators for kids. The Sunday comics can become wrapping paper for children's gifts. There are ways to squeeze more mileage out of everything from aquarium water and Ziploc bags to adding machine tapes and pickle juice. (Whew!)

Creative thrift means that rather than do without, use a homemade version. Homemade greeting cards, invitations, ornaments, note paper, and wrapping paper are less expensive than those at the Hallmark store. Many varieties of toys can be made at home. Handmade gifts such as wreaths, calligraphy art, or jellies and jams are not only inexpensive to give, but also more appreciated by most recipients. Even dog biscuits, baby wipes, crackers, Play Doh, baby food, and cleaning solution can be made inexpensively at home. (Some of these recipes are in the *Tightwad Gazette*.)

Creative thrift means that rather than do without, we make smart major changes. You may be sitting on top of a gold mine, in terms of changes you could make that would yield huge savings. Only you can determine whether major changes are cost-effective enough to be worth the trouble. Would it be worth moving to a smaller home to lower your mortgage payment by a few hundred dollars a month? What about refinancing? Could you lower or eliminate a car payment if you sold your BMW and replaced it with a Ford? Would you benefit by selling something (land, equipment, a condo, or a rental property) and investing the money elsewhere?

PICTURE THIS!

If a season at home seems remote to you for financial reasons, read this section again and imagine yourself putting these ideas into practice. One idea, by itself, probably will not make it possible for you to be at home. But the combination of several ideas could result in a lifestyle that would easily change your stay-at-home bottom line from red to black.

A Caveat. No matter how zealous you may be to reduce expenditures, there are some areas that should not be cut. *Never* scrimp in an area that could compromise health or safety. In an effort to cut corners, some people make their own contact lens saline solution. Because they cannot insure the sterility of their product, some of these people have suffered eye infections or loss of vision as a result. Don't risk a tragedy to save a few dollars.

Similarly, you may come across recipes for homemade infant formula. These may be economical, but they may not be sufficiently nutritious for your baby. Check with your pediatrician first and follow his or her instructions precisely. If you buy baby furniture, toys, or car seats second hand, be positive they are safe before you put them into use.

Remember the love-is-meeting-needs theme? Be a wise and loving need-meeter, even when money is in short supply. Never cut back in areas of genuine need or preventative health care such as prescription medications, dental checkups, annual Pap tests, psychotherapy, speech therapy, and well-baby checkups.

You can exercise prudent, creative thrift in these areas without compromising quality care. Ask your doctor about generic medications. Discuss the possibility of spacing therapy sessions further apart. See if your dentist thinks your family would do just as well with checkups every nine months as they do with visits every six months.

Keep in mind that one family's luxury is another family's necessity. Only the family itself can determine the difference! For years, my husband's job included an erratic schedule and frequent travel. As a result, he could not maintain our lawn. Our lot has a significant slope to it, which meant that I couldn't take care of it either. It is very difficult for me at 110 pounds to handle a power mower on sloping terrain. Realizing that my chances for flipping the mower and landing in the emergency room were excellent, we opted to hire a professional lawn service. In North Carolina, grass grows five or six months out of a year. Lawn care costs about $100 a month—$600 a year—but it has not been an optional expense for us.

DECISIONS

As promised, here is a suggested agenda for discussing finances and economical living, with a view toward a season at home.

Preparation for Discussion

Complete the two-month spending log, as described in step three, above. Determine your essential and optional expenses with your spouse prior to this discussion.

Agenda for Discussion

I. Tithing
   A. How do you feel about the idea of tithing your income?
   B. If you are uncomfortable with tithing, would you be open to starting this practice in order to test God (Malachi 3:10)?
   C. If you have been tithing for a long time, how would you feel about increasing your tithe as a demonstration of your trust in God's ability to provide for you during a season at home?
II. Planning Ahead
   A. Debt
      1. If you are currently in debt, what is the total amount you owe? How long will it take you to pay back these debts, using your current strategy? What, if anything, could be done to pay off these debts more quickly?
      2. Will debt keep you from a season at home? If so, are you open to seeking advice from an

146

organization such as Consumer Credit Counseling?

3. If you are not currently in debt, how could you structure your spending during a season at home to avoid accumulating debt?

B. Savings/Living on One Income

1. How much money do you currently have in savings and investments? How much of this would be available in case of emergencies if your family had to, or chose to, live on one income?

2. How much money would you like to have in savings before beginning a season at home?

3. What changes in your spending patterns would enable you to save more money?

4. If both spouses are working: Do you think it is realistic to begin living on one income and saving the other? If not, are there any lifestyle changes you could implement that would make this possible?

5. In your situation, is there merit to having the father be the at-home parent? If so, how do you feel about this?

C. Investigating Work-at-Home Options

1. Do you think it may be necessary for the at-home parent to earn money by working at home at some point?

2. If so, how can present employment contacts best be tapped for leads that will be helpful when that time comes?

III. Assess Current Spending

A. Do you think your spending log accurately reflects the way your family spends money? If not, why not?

B. How do you feel about the way your family spends money?

C. If your family made no changes in its spending habits, could you afford a season at home?

D. If both parents work: According to your spending log, what are the second wage earner's work-related costs?

E. Do you feel that, for your family, having both parents work is cost effective?

IV. Economizing

A. Based on your spending log, how much does your family spend each month on essential goods and services? How much on optional goods and services?

B. What spending cuts could most easily be made in these areas? What lifestyle changes are in order? (Use the text as a springboard to discussion, if needed.)

C. How could you economize creatively, so that family members would not feel deprived? Highlight ideas in the text that seem good to you and discuss these with your spouse.

D. If you eliminated and reduced as much as possible, how much would be saved?

E. After making cuts, is there still a gap between income and expenses? What could you do to bridge this gap?

NINE

Working at Home

A mother with a talent or a skill who can make money using it, should.
—Shannon, work-at-home mother of three

Not every woman who stays at home needs to become a work-at-home mom. But for many mothers, working at home is the key that unlocks the door to a season at home. Even after a family has committed itself to tithing, planned ahead as much as possible, assessed their spending, and economized as much as is practical for them, there may still be a gap between their cost of living and take-home pay. When there is, working at home may be the best option. This chapter is devoted to that option, the fifth and final step in the stay-at-home financial strategy.

A GROWING TREND

Working at home is a trend that is growing. Twenty-six million people now work at home at least part-time. (That's 10 percent of the population.)[1] Research indicates that by the middle of this decade, 44 percent of all U.S. households will have a home office.[2] LINK Resources, a Manhattan-based research company, estimates that by 1995 there may be more

149

than eleven million telecommuters—company employees who work at home but stay connected to their office via a computer terminal.[3] Many of these home business people are mothers, working at home in order to be with their children during their formative years. According to research reported by the authors of *Staying Home*, 22 percent of all working women now work out of their homes.[4]

While most mothers I surveyed for this book identified themselves as at-home mothers, slightly more than one-third of them (eleven women) were earning some income while at home. To supplement the surveys, I conducted personal interviews with four other mothers who run successful at-home businesses. These surveys and interviews provided a wealth of information about earning money during a season at home.

My sample revealed that working at home has three variations: (1) work done entirely at home, (2) work based at home with an out-of-the-home component, and (3) part-time work done away from home but with an at-home component. Here is a brief description of each category.

Work Done Entirely at Home. Work in this category occurs entirely within the home itself. This set-up is what usually comes to mind when people talk about working at home.

There are a multitude of ways to earn money without leaving your house. Some of these involve the telephone: doing telephone surveys, dispatching medical or repair personnel, or fund-raising, for example. Other jobs require a computer: women with a proficiency in a foreign language can translate and transcribe legal, sales, or scientific documents at home. Some women use computers to do medical transcription, compile newsletters for clients, or work as free-lance writers.

Craftswomen and artists can work at home, too. Here are just some of the possibilities: knitting or macramé, doll making, silk-screen, graphic design, sewing draperies or custom-made clothing, making garment alterations, calligraphy, sweatshirt painting, making Christmas ornaments, woodworking, pet grooming, upholstering, and furniture refinishing.

Some women make money by using their home's square footage: providing child care or giving lessons to individuals and groups (piano or voice lessons, academic tutoring, cooking classes for kids, instruction in crafts).

These ways of earning money have one thing in common: the endeavor takes place entirely at home.

Mary Howe, thirty-three, has a true work-at-home job. Drawing upon her years of professional experience, Mary started an in-home marketing company that provides prospect qualification services. ("That's finding potential customers for our clients," she explained.) Mary and a friend, another at-home mother, work in tandem. For each client, they design a telephone calling script which will identify potential customers for that business.

"My friend spends an hour a day in her kitchen doing phone calls," said Mary. When her friend is successful in identifying prospects, she passes the baton to Mary, who does the follow-up: "I enter things into our data base and send out letters to clients—the kind of thing I can do on a Saturday morning or when the kids are in bed."

Mary's work is *demand driven*, which means that it does not always fall neatly into child-free hours. Sometimes she must work surrounded by her three children. "We've got a basket of toys and a TV in the office," she said. Working in the midst of children can sometimes be trying. "They'll be bouncing off the walls while I'm sitting at the computer trying to get work done," she admitted. But overall, Mary is pleased with her work-at-home arrangements. "This is real flexible," she said. "I'm only working five to eight hours a week." As for the future? "I anticipate growing. I don't ever want to work full-time while I've got kids in school."

Work Based at Home With an Outside Component. This is at-home work with a twist. Part of the work occurs at home and part of the work occurs somewhere else—most often at the home of a customer.

Businesses that rely on home parties for customer

contacts fall into this category. So does work which involves delivering a product to a customer. The product could be homemade or it could be something manufactured by a company, such as Avon's cosmetics. Many goods are sold this way—cookware, jewelry, decorative accessories, lingerie, encyclopedias, Tupperware, and children's clothes, to name a few.

Karen Coalson, thirty-two, came up with a home-based business idea which has allowed her to be at home with her two girls for five years. "The name of my business," said Karen, "is Say It with Signs, Baskets, and Balloons."

At first, Karen's business simply offered signs that could be rented and placed in yards for special occasions: stork signs for new mothers, and clown signs for children's birthdays. Without intending for the business to grow, Karen explained, it did: "People started calling me and saying, 'Do you do balloons?' 'Do you do baskets?' 'Do you do this or that?' and it just clicked. Everything fell into place, and I started adding on."

Today, customers find Karen's business through an ad in the Yellow Pages and by picking up her business card from local OB-GYN offices. She offers an assortment of gift baskets and balloon bouquets in addition to the signs. "Usually whatever people call and ask for, I try to do for them," she said.

Say It with Signs, Baskets, and Balloons has become a family operation. Karen's husband, Gregg, helps out: "He blows up the balloons. He helps me deliver, sometimes. He watches the girls while I do my deliveries." The Coalson children enjoy the business, too, sometimes accompanying their mom on afternoon deliveries (most are done in the morning while the girls are in school and preschool). "They enjoy the balloons and watching me," observed Karen. "My daughter Amy says that this is what she wants to do when she grows up, and that makes me feel good."

Karen's business continues to expand as her children get older. Recently she's begun to decorate for weddings and rehearsals. But does she ever think about returning to a full-time job? "I have thought about it," she admitted. "But it would hurt me to have to go back to work. My kids beg me to stay at home. Amy says: 'Mommy, you *have* a job. You work at home and you have me and Laura to look after.' That hits me hard. I've sat and imagined going to pick up my children from a day care. I just cannot. I feel very blessed that I could stay at home."

Part-time Work with an At-Home Component. At first this category may be hard to comprehend. One might think that if all the work is done away from home then it's a part-time job. Well, not exactly. It's the at-home component that prompts me to distinguish this kind of work from other part-time jobs. Many jobs in this category are a bit out of the ordinary.

Bonny's job is a good example. It is a part-time job, but not a typical one. Between 4:00 a.m. and 6:00 a.m. Monday through Friday, while her husband and children are asleep, Bonny delivers newspapers. Her job is practically invisible to her family. ("Because they are asleep, I don't really think it affects them that much," Bonny said.) Bonny earns $700 a month this way, and the money is a big help.

The at-home part of Bonny's job is paperwork. This consumes only a few hours of her time each week, creating what she considers to be a practically ideal job: "To me, it seems impossible for anyone to work at home with small children. The best thing about my job is that when it's done, it's done. I have guaranteed pay, and we have less stress because of the extra $700 a month."

Child care is usually no problem for Bonny because her kids are at home with dad, asleep. "There have been one or two occasions when my children had to go with me because my husband was out of town," she said. "They loved it! It was like a big adventure or a camp-out to them." Bonny, twenty-eight, is a former Wachovia personal banker. She has chosen to keep her newspaper route a secret: only her family knows her early morning whereabouts. "To me," she reflected, "it's a private thing." It's also an answer to prayer: "I remember praying, 'Lord, I need a job that doesn't

153

interfere with my family and pays at least $500 a month.'. . .I didn't think there was such a job—but I believe the Lord provided this work just for me."

Wendy and Kerri also have part-time jobs with an at-home component. They are nurses who make home visits, and they work on an on-call basis. They get the benefit of staying at home in exchange for a commitment to be available if they are needed.

Wendy, whose children are ages three and one, works only three to four hours every other week. When she is on call she wears a pager so she can respond to questions over the phone. On rare occasions, she has to leave home during the evening. When she must make a visit she performs nursing tasks like drawing blood or changing a catheter. Wendy makes about $580 a month. She could make more, but she has decided to limit her work. "Anything over one day a week becomes frustrating for me and gets me out of balance. My ironing mounts up, we eat out too much, I'm irritable, the house becomes grade C."

Kerri is employed by Hospice. She is on call in the evenings and logs about thirty hours at work each week. Kerri used to have a full-time nursing job, but she likes her present arrangement much better. "When I am at home, on call, I can pick up my kids [ages seven and twelve] at school, care for my house, and volunteer at school."

THE LET'S-GET-REAL SIDE OF AT-HOME WORK

Work-at-home success stories abound. But if you get depressed when you hear them, you are probably a mother of preschoolers. Let's get real. There are additional considerations which come into play during children's early years.

During the red- and yellow-light years, the physical demands of children, the constant interruptions, and the exhaustion inherent to mothering young children can make running a home business challenging. Many women who leave their jobs to stay at home when their babies are born become extremely discouraged when they discover that working from home is not as easy as they expected it to be. First-time parents may greatly underestimate the time and energy that infants, toddlers, and preschoolers require.

Mothering young children is different than mothering older children from a depletion-of-maternal-resources point of view. As has been noted, 42 percent of the women responding to one survey indicated that they spent fourteen or more hours a day caring for their children. As I contemplated the length of mothers' workdays, I wondered, When could they do an at-home job? The same question came to mind when I read in *Staying Home* that "child care can expand to fill all your waking hours."[5]

Many moms in the trenches bear witness to this reality. Kate, who has older children as well as a two-year-old, said, "I feel that it would be difficult to earn money at home due to the time and attention it would take. I already feel exhausted—I can't imagine adding another activity." Lisa's children are ages ten, eight, and two. Over the years she has done bookkeeping and sewing at home. In her opinion, "Working at home is *very* difficult with small children and almost always creates more frustration."

None of this is to say that working at home cannot be done, or that it should not be done with small children at your feet. Kate said, "I can understand doing it if it meant a choice between earning money at home or going back to work." And that, of course, is exactly why many moms work at home.

The Voice of Experience

I interviewed two very successful work-at-home veterans in order to learn from their experience. Both of these mothers began their at-home jobs when their children were very small, and both have been in business for more than a decade. How did they manage to work at home when their children were with them all day? How had their businesses changed as their children grew? I decided to find out.

Beverly Turner. Beverly's job falls into the work-based-at-home category. She works for Discovery Toys, a network marketing company that carries educational toys for everyone from newborns to adults. Beverly has been with this company for more than ten years and today enjoys senior manager status.

Beverly described herself as an independent contractor. As such, her work provides two things that she said were "more important than anything else when I started." Those things are control and flexibility.

About ten years ago, Beverly needed a work schedule she could control because she was breast-feeding her infant son, Jonathan. "I did want to work completely around that schedule," she said. So, at first, she worked "on a *very* part-time basis." She said, "I just did what I could, and that's the way I started."

A former speech and language pathologist, Beverly noted that, unlike her former profession, her work-from-home career has been amazingly flexible. "I have found that whatever schedule I have needed to work around, I have been able to do that successfully with this business. . . . For example, when Jonathan was at home almost all the time, I had just one day a week when a lady came in and helped me with child care and housekeeping. I was able to work mainly that one day doing the things outside my home that I needed to do." During her son's early years, Beverly chose to work only a few hours a week even though she was "overwhelmed with business from the very beginning."

As her child grew, Beverly expanded her business. "When my son began a preschool program," she said, "I found that I was able to do more and more things during the daytime. Women could have a brunch with their friends while their children were at preschool, and I would set up my toys and have a demonstration."

Beverly adjusted her schedule again when her son reached school age. When public school "just didn't work" for Jonathan, Beverly began to teach him at home. "When I started home schooling," she explained, "I found that I needed to be home a lot more during the day. Because I didn't have that daytime flexibility anymore, I was able to shift my business successfully to evenings." Beverly still home schools, but now that her son is older and involved in many outside activities, she has rearranged her schedule again, dividing her time between day and evening hours.

Beverly has given her son, Jonathan, who is now eleven, a role in her business. He accompanies Beverly to her in-home toy demonstration parties. "He's a wonderful worker," boasted his mom. "I pay him, and it's been so good in so many ways. It's been excellent for maturing him."

After so many years in business, Beverly's financial rewards have become substantial. "The people that you sponsor in the business become your direct recruits," she said, "and because of the training you provide for them, the company will send you an override check, which is a certain percentage of what these people sell."

Knowing this, I asked Beverly if she ever saw herself going back to a forty-hour-a-week job working for somebody else. "Are you crazy?" she responded playfully. "I didn't make this amount working full-time with a master's degree and several years experience as a speech pathologist!"

Mary Bollinger. We met Mary briefly in chapter six. Mary's job is also in the work-based-at-home category. For the past eleven years, Mary has done medical transcription at home for local physicians. While the bulk of her work takes place at the keyboard, Mary also picks up and delivers work daily. When she first started her at-home transcription business, Mary was married and the mother of a three-year-old. Today she is a single parent who continues to work at home in order to have more time with her fourteen-year-old son (also named Jonathan).

Mary recalled how she got her business started. She and her husband realized that they "couldn't make ends meet and we needed my income," but Mary also knew that she "wanted to be an at-home mom, full-time." So, Mary began to pray: "Lord, I don't want to go back to work and be a full-time working mother and put Jonathan in day care." She asked God for "leadership and guidance in what to do."

It soon dawned on Mary that she had a skill that every doctor's office needed. But what she didn't know was whether she could use that skill at home. "At the time,' she said, "I had only heard that people worked at home. I didn't actually know anyone who did." She put an ad in the newspaper, "just to see what would happen." What happened was work! "That's how I got my first job," she said. "From there, word of mouth spread that I was doing this from home and I picked up other things." Looking back, Mary reflected, "I really believe that the idea to put that ad in the paper was God leading me to do that."

In the beginning, Mary worked three hours a day, mostly while Jonathan was asleep. "With very small children," she said, "it's hard to work from home and give [your children] the time they need, and yet meet your deadlines." As her son got older, Mary increased her hours. But when she did, it became more difficult to work: "He napped less, so that meant there were fewer hours for me to work." To accomplish her work, Mary had to rely on some ingenious methods.

Today, Mary typically works ten to twelve hours a day, making it necessary to continue devising ingenious methods to meet her deadlines. She gets up very early in the morning to spend time in Scripture and to put in at least an hour of typing before Jonathan wakes up. After Mary sees her son off to school, she may do some housecleaning or go back to typing.

Mary works until it's time to make her afternoon delivery and pick Jonathan up from school. Back at home, Mary and Jonathan spend fifteen or twenty minutes together before Mary goes back to work. Late in the afternoon, she makes a final delivery. Then she and Jonathan share supper and spend time talking. Before falling into bed, Mary will put in two or three more hours of typing.

That kind of schedule would surely do many moms in! But Mary said, "When you have to survive by doing this, you can make yourself do it real easy!" And, she's used to it: "Since 1988 that's the type of schedule I've kept. When I had to work more hours to get bills paid, I would only sleep four hours a night. But this is the way life is right now, being a single mom, to have enough money to meet the bills."

Does she ever anticipate a nine-to-five job outside the home? "I don't foresee that," replied Mary. Instead, she plans to keep working at home, "until my son gets off to college, no matter how weird the schedule is."

WORKING AT HOME: IS IT FOR YOU?

Companies that employ at-home workers recognize that such jobs are not for everyone. One company, The Linton Factor, Inc., employs a clinical psychologist to administer pre-employment screening tests. These tests "determine who is psychologically capable of working in an isolated, self-managed situation."[6]

What about you? Are you well-suited for working a strictly at-home job? Would you like it? Here's a test: How are you doing as a stay-at-home mom? Full-time mothering and working at home have some important things in common. To better judge how you are doing, ask yourself the following questions:

1. How do you like being your own boss? Do you like calling the shots—determining what will be done and when it will be done?
2. Are you enjoying autonomy and flexibility? Or would you feel more relaxed and secure in a job that provides you with boundaries: defined responsibilities, specified working hours, and pre-determined compensation?
3. Are you reasonably organized?
4. Are you a self-disciplined, self-directed person—an internally motivated self-starter?
5. Do you possess a don't-quit attitude? Are you hard to discourage?
6. Do you enjoy working alone or are you happier working with, or around, other people?

Use your experience at home to determine the answers—and tell yourself the truth! An honest appraisal will help you decide whether you are cut out for working at home or whether you'd be happier in a home-based job that provides more contact with other people. A second opinion is also valuable. Your husband knows you well; ask him to answer these same questions about you.

Prayer is very important at this stage. Working at home is a big commitment of time, talent, and energy. Go forward only when you have the confidence that undertaking a home job is what God wants you to do. All four work-at-home mothers I interviewed, and several of those I surveyed, could point to ways that God had paved the way for their home businesses. Surrender all your options to him, and *expect* his direction.

Advice from Work-at-Home Moms

I asked some work-at-home moms what advice they would give to a mother considering the idea of working at home. They mentioned two things.

Go for It! Karen Coalson said, "If somebody wants to stay at home and work out of their home, I say go for it." She advised that such women set goals, make a financial plan, and pray about it. Similarly, Mary Bollinger wanted women to know, "It's not impossible." She feels that, "It's worth being able to be with your kids to work crazy schedules, weird hours, and work around all the problems."

Start Small and Be Realistic. Realize that your business will grow as your children get older. Realize, too, that an at-home job will require some of the time and energy that you would otherwise be devoting to other responsibilities. Michelle said, "The time I spend tutoring and keeping older children after school takes time away from my kids." Mary Howe was one of several moms who said, "The more you work, the less time you have to keep your house." Nobody can do it all. To avoid a perpetual sense of guilt, establish your priorities and arrange your day around them.

She's Back! (The Work-at-Home Super Mom)

Moms who work at home and *don't* establish priorities are at risk for burnout. "It is realistic to earn money at home as long as you don't lose sight of why you're home in the first place," twenty-eight-year-old Kris told me. "I've known mothers who decided to baby-sit small children in their home and found they were spreading themselves so thin that their own children weren't getting the quality time they deserved. This defeated their decision to stay home."

Kris knows about burnout from personal experience, too. "I sell specialty cakes out of my home," she explained. "I once tried to do ten the week before Christmas. I became drained and irritable. I was staying up until after midnight in order to meet my deadlines, and it is important to get a full night's rest when dealing with toddlers! So, I learned to put things in better perspective so I can give the very best of me to my child." Now Kris tries to limit herself to making two to three cakes a week.

Working at home is a learning experience. It takes time to learn to balance this combination of responsibilities. When a work-at-home mom sets her goals too high or overcommits herself, she may find herself so spent that her children don't benefit from her being at home. When this happens, working at home is as out of sync with the seasons of life as working away from home. It's the Super-Mom myth all over again, with a new coat of hearth-and-home paint. The work-at-home mom may change her workplace, but she still may be trying to do it all.

Keep in mind that at-home jobs, like other jobs, must fit you. Said Mary Howe, "I'm the only one who knows how much I can handle and still do my primary duty, which is to be a wife and a mother." Be wise—and be realistic—don't become a work-at-home Super Mom.

Here's Help

If you are going to work at home before your children are in school, keep these important guidelines in mind.

Know Your Child. The first important variable that can affect your success is your child. Some preschoolers are dynamos of non-stop energy. They are constantly in motion, into everything, wreaking havoc everywhere they go. They may be incapable of entertaining themselves for more than five minutes at a time. Mothers of these children may take an understandably dim view of working at home. Other children are more passive and relaxed, content to play by themselves for long periods of time, or just happy to keep mom company while she works at the computer or sews.

My friend, Candy, has a daughter like this. While Candy works at the computer putting together newsletters for various organizations, her three-year-old daughter spends hours in her own imaginary world, playing with the doll family who lives in her big doll house. Candy is always available to her daughter and her schedule is extremely flexible. Working at home is feasible for Candy, partly due to her daughter's personality and the fact that she is content to play alone.

If you are the mother of many children, working at home will be more difficult. Charesa, who has four children ages eight, six, four, and two, has learned that even volunteer jobs can be an overload. "I find I stay up late at night to prepare or to catch up on work," she said, "and then I am not my best the next day. I can't do two things well at once."

Choose Your Work Carefully. The second important variable is the kind of work you want to do. Cami noted, "Finding the right thing to do is the tough part." Mary Howe said that ideally, an at-home job should be "something you could do with your children present." Something that even "with their noise and commotion you could still get the work done."

Certain kinds of work are easier to do at home than others. Work that can be picked up and put down over and over throughout the day may be easier to do than work that must be completed in one sitting or has materials or equipment that are expensive, fragile, or even dangerous to a small child.

If you want to work at home but are not sure what kind of work would be best for you, check these books out at your local library. (If your library doesn't have them call a large chain bookstore in your area.):

• *1001 Businesses You Can Start From Home: The World's Most Complete Directory of Part-Time and Full-Time Business Ideas, Including Start-up Costs, Marketing Tips, Sources of Information*, by Daryl Allen Hall (John Wiley & Sons, Inc.: 1992).

• *The Work-at-Home Sourcebook: How to Find "At Home" Work That's Right for You*, by Lynie Arden (Live Oak Publications, Boulder, Colorado: 1987).

Get a Sitter, If Your Work Requires One. Lisa said, "I feel that if working at home is an option, child care is also needed, or else there is too much conflict." Bernadette Grey, the editor of *Home Computing* magazine, advised a pregnant, work-at-home writer to seriously consider hiring a sitter after her baby was born. She said, "Speaking from experience, it's really impossible to do both."[7]

When a mother's at-home job requires sustained concentration or mandates that she seclude herself to get her work done, she will find it difficult to work at home apart from the help of a regular baby-sitter during the red- and yellow-light phases. It can be, as Holly put it, "next to impossible to get a home job done while the children are underfoot."

When mothers of infants, toddlers, or preschoolers have the help of a baby-sitter, working at home is much easier—but the cost of child care can eat into profits. One way to avoid the expense of a sitter is to exchange child care with other moms. Another strategy is to rely on family members, whenever possible. And if the husband can be the one to care for the children while the wife works at home, that's a plus for everyone. (A twenty-six-year study shows that father-care—giving baths, meals, and basic care—more than twice a week fosters empathy and compassion in children.[8])

Enlist Your Spouse's Support. Your husband's support and encouragement are essential to your success in any at-home business. Depending upon your business, your husband may have to take a more active role if you are to succeed. Discussing his role in your business ahead of time can ward off misunderstanding and conflict. Here are some questions that you should ask him *before* you start a home business:

1. On a scale of one to ten, how excited are you about my working at home? (One means not excited at all; ten means very excited.) Can you tell me why you feel this way?
2. What problems do you anticipate? How do you think we should handle these?
3. What do you think are the good points about my working at home?
4. Are you willing to provide child care when it is needed?
5. Would you run errands (such as deliver work or products to a client, pick up supplies, and buy groceries)? Do some housework and cooking? Work along with me, if I need help meeting a deadline?
6. Are you willing to help on a regular basis? On an as-needed basis?

HOW TO GET STARTED

If you determine that working at home is for you, and if your spouse is with you in the venture, here are some tips on how to get started.

Embark on a Fact-Finding Mission

You need to arm yourself with preparatory information and learn as much as you can about your work before you actually begin. (Of course, you'll continue to learn along the way from practical experience.) To get started, make three important phone calls.

Call Your County or State Cooperative Extension Service. This agency can provide many printed resource materials and give suggestions about other kinds of local services you could utilize. When I called, I received many helpful things by return mail: a work sheet for doing market research and brochures entitled, "Starting a Business: Know The Law," "A Business of Your Own: Decision-Making," "Planning Your Home Office," and "Marketing Your Craft."

Call the U.S. Small Business Administration Answer Desk in Washington, D.C. Their toll-free number is 1-800-827-5722. Follow the recorded prompts to get the information you need. This phone call can provide information in many areas, such as: starting your own business, financing your own business, where to get local counseling and training, women's business ownership, and minority small businesses.

Call the Local Chamber of Commerce. This organization can tell you everything you need to know about local licensing and tax laws, as well as other specific things you may need to know. For example, depending on the kind of business you have in mind, you may want to know how to register the name of your business, how to incorporate, or how to be licensed to operate a home day care. The Winston-Salem, N.C., Chamber of Commerce offers a new business start-up kit which is available free of charge at the public library. Your chamber may have something similar. Ask!

Go to the Library. If your library has an Info Trak or ProQuest, type in *home-based businesses* to search among hundreds of relevant articles which have appeared in recent periodicals. You can print out the articles and take them home to read. (If you need help using Info Trak or ProQuest, ask a librarian.) If your library does not have either of these databases, you can use *The Reader's Guide to Periodical Literature* to accomplish the same thing.

While you are at the library, look for pamphlets and books about your intended business or working at home. (Some suggested titles appear in Appendix B at the end of this book.) Armed with a wealth of information from many sources, you will be able to continue to pray intelligently as you begin your venture.

Begin to Establish a Network of Support

If you know of other mothers who work at home, phone them and ask questions. Even better, meet with them personally. If you find several work-at-home moms in your area, consider organizing into a support group that meets on a regular basis.

There are some national organizations that might be helpful to you. One is the Association of Part-Time Professionals. APTP publishes a newsletter, *Working Options*, and offers a part-timer's resource kit, which addresses home-based business concerns. You can contact them at:

Crescent Plaza
Suite 216
7700 Leesburg Pike
Falls Church, Virginia 22043
(703) 734-7975

Self-employed people can pool their resources to obtain benefits such as dental and health insurance, or discounts on services such as fax or legal help. If you are interested in investigating this, contact the organizations below. Upon request, you will receive an information packet and an application. (You may need to obtain a tax number in order to participate.):

The National Business Association
1-800-456-0440

The National Independent Business League
1-800-683-0575

While considering a home-based career, remember the words of Paul in Colossians 3:23–24: "Whatever you do, work at it with all your heart, as working for the Lord, not for men, since you know that you will receive an inheritance from the Lord as a reward. It is the Lord Christ you are serving."

TEN

Survival Kit

I've held two professional jobs, and being at home with a two-year-old all day is by far the hardest work I've ever done.
  —Kris, twenty-eight, mother of one son

A few years ago aboard a jet bound for Los Angeles, I learned something about good parenting.

My son, who was two at the time, was flying with me. Maybe it was Christopher's presence in the next seat that made me pay close attention to the flight attendant's safety pitch prior to takeoff. Her instructions about seat-belt buckles, locating emergency exits, and turning the seat cushions into flotation devices sounded familiar. But when she described how the oxygen masks would drop down in front of us should there be a loss of cabin pressure, something about her instructions suddenly seemed peculiar to me. She said that anyone traveling with a small child should put on his or her own oxygen mask before attempting to assist the child.

As I envisioned such a scenario, it bothered me. If Chris and I both needed oxygen, wouldn't it be selfish to take care of myself first? What might happen to him while I fumbled with my mask? In a crisis, shouldn't I place my child's safety above my own?

I thought about this for a while before concluding that the airline knew what it was talking about. I reasoned that if there were a loss of cabin pressure sufficient to cause the masks to drop, a child might panic or begin to cry, making it difficult for a parent to get the mask over the child's head. While the parent was trying to win the power struggle, he or she might pass out from lack of oxygen. Then, with no one to help, the child would pass out, too. As a result, neither parent nor child would have their needs met. But by instructing the parent to do the "selfish" thing and place his or her own mask on first, the airline increases the likelihood that the child's needs will be met, as well.

The lesson I learned that day is this: it's not selfish for mothers to get their own needs met; it's smart. When our needs are met, we do a better job at parenting. If we don't take care of ourselves, we have more difficulty taking care of our children. What's more, the concept of "love is meeting needs" applies to ourselves, as well. Jesus said that the second greatest commandment was, "Love your neighbor as yourself" (Matthew 22:39). In order to meet our own needs, every stay-at-home mom needs a seven-item survival kit.

SURVIVAL KIT ITEM #1: TAKE CARE OF YOURSELF

Everyone has needs; it's part of being human. So it's normal for mothers to have needs. It's okay to acknowledge them to yourself, to God, and to your family and friends. What's more, it's okay to get your needs met. If this seems too obvious, remember that many mothers become so engulfed in the task of meeting the physical and emotional needs of their families that they seriously neglect themselves.

Mothers frequently hit the ground running. It's not that unusual for a busy mom to forget to eat lunch or to find that it's dinner time and she never found time to brush her hair or put in her contact lenses, let alone read the Bible or do something for fun.

Every at-home mother has days like this. It's inevitable; it goes with the territory. (If you haven't experienced a day like this yet, don't worry—you will!) The caution I want to give is this: too many days like this will deplete your resources. You can burn out, either physically, mentally, emotionally, or spiritually. Burnout is not only bad for you, but it's bad for your kids and bad for your marriage, as well.

To avoid burnout, treat yourself well. You are not only the anchor of your family; you are an important person in your own right. You count, and your needs are important. When you feel irritable, anxious, or depressed, stop and ask yourself an important question: What do I need right now? When you identify the need, plan a way to meet it.

Everyone has at least six basic needs: emotional, physical, social, intellectual, spiritual, and creative. But what meets a need for one woman may make another miserable. Some women find sewing relaxing and enjoyable, and it meets a creative need for them. Others find it stressful and irritating. Many women enjoy talking with friends on the phone, but some women avoid the phone as much as possible, preferring face-to-face conversation.

Each woman must take a personal inventory of her unique set of needs and determine how those needs are best met. The common constraints, of course, are lack of child care, lack of money, and lack of time. The worst villain of all, however, may be guilt—the feeling that you don't deserve fun, relaxation, or time alone. If taking care of your needs makes you feel selfish, remind yourself that you'll be a better mom if you give yourself the time to recharge and relax. You must give priority to your own needs, at least in some areas, at least occasionally. Some sage (probably a child) once observed, "If mama ain't happy, ain't *nobody* happy." There's a lot of truth embedded in that humor. Since mama is the emotional climate control of the home, it's important for her to be happy!

Finding Time for Yourself. I asked the women in my

survey about their strategies for finding time alone and enjoying life. Some, like Sandra, who works as a housekeeper during her daughter's preschool hours, admitted, "I never do have time for myself." Similarly, April said, "I really don't have any good strategies for finding time for myself." Some answered my question about finding time for themselves by explaining that during their children's nap time they clean the house. That's not what I call time for yourself!

Those moms who did find time for themselves used four common strategies. Dee spoke for most of these women when she eloquently described the first strategy: "Nap time, nap time, nap time!" Paula said she used nap times "to write letters, read, sew, and cook, which are things that help me feel worthwhile."

Mary Ann makes use of strategies two and three: getting up early and mother's morning out programs. Mary Ann's daughter goes to mother's morning out once a week, between 9:00 a.m. and noon.

Strategy four is daddy-care. "Time for myself has been easy for me because my husband wants to have his time with our daughter," Rebecca said. "He keeps her sometimes two or three times per week so that I can do things I want to do."

Holly shared similar sentiments: "My husband takes care of my son one night a week so that I can be in our church choir. I often ask him to take our son for a few hours on the weekend so that I can have some time to myself."

The authors of *Staying Home* suggested a fifth strategy: establish a daily quitting time, just as if you had a paid job outside the home. Of course, you can't go off duty as far as your children are concerned, but you can draw the line on housework and begin to attend to some of your own needs.

Many mothers find that small pleasures in small doses can work wonders. Hiring a high school girl for an hour or two a week can help rejuvenate a weary mom. This small amount of time is enough to take a hot bath, to make a phone call to a friend, or to quietly cross stitch. Many women whose husbands don't or can't help much with child care and who have no family close by swap child care with friends. Others join or start baby-sitting co-ops in their neighborhoods or churches.

Looking Good. Cami said, "I struggle with self-esteem. I just don't feel like I even look good at all most of the time. My hair looks horrible . . . I can't dress like I used to."

Like Cami, many moms at home find that their appearance has a direct bearing on how they feel about themselves. More than one formerly well-dressed professional woman has come home for a season, only to look in the mirror one morning and discover she could be nominated as poster child for the fashion-impaired!

If the appearance of your hair, makeup, and clothing contributes to your sense of well-being, give yourself permission to pamper yourself. Good grooming need not be expensive, and moms at home can look great in jogging suits and jeans. Looking good usually requires only a little extra time, effort, and creativity.

If you sew, make inexpensive, comfortable, casual clothes you like. You can often find quality clothing in good repair at consignment and thrift shops as well.

You can make the most of your natural attributes by discovering your season's color palette. For a one-time investment of money, you can determine whether your skin tone and hair are best showcased by spring, summer, autumn, or winter colors. (Why not ask for a color analysis for your birthday or for Christmas?) Wearing the right colors can make a surprising difference.

Almost anything looks better with a touch of color— including moms. A hint of blush or a bit of eyeliner can brighten your attitude as well as your appearance. Some moms do a quick touch-up every day just before their husbands get home from work.

What do you need? Whatever it is, plan a strategy for getting those needs met. Remind yourself that there is a lot of sacrifice involved in staying at home, just as there is a lot of sacrifice involved in working outside the home—but the difference is that when mom is at home, the adult, not the child, is making the larger sacrifice. That alone entitles you to some time off!

SURVIVAL KIT ITEM #2:
CREATE A STRONG SUPPORT SYSTEM

Society's structure has changed so rapidly that our mother-support system has all but evaporated. At-home moms may find themselves hundreds or even thousands of miles away from the mothers, sisters, aunts, and grandmothers who, in an earlier time, would have provided companionship and help with child care. Old friends may be close in heart but far away geographically, while the women who live down the street spend their days at work.

As a result, many women who stay at home do so without the encouragement, companionship, and tangible help that the job of full-time mothering requires—help that was readily available to women in previous generations. Because of this, many mothers find a season at home to be an exhausting, lonely, difficult chore. No wonder so many women give up and go to work! Don't let this happen to you—find a support system.

An Essential Ingredient. Friendship and companionship are legitimate needs—needs God never intended to go unmet. Meeting these important needs is not selfish; it's essential to the success of a season at home. Studies have shown that when moms have good support systems, they interact with their children in more positive ways. A 1991 article published in *Child Development* reported these findings:

> Mothers with more supportive networks presumably have more of their emotional needs met and thus are better able to meet the emotional needs of their children. Consequently, they are able to be warm while simultaneously facilitating their children's autonomy by allowing their children to control their own activities. Previous research has shown that mothers who are

172

satisfied with their networks do report a greater sense of well-being.[1]

Ideally, every mother's support system will include her husband, her extended family, her neighbors, her church family, and her friends. Friends are especially important to women who may not have extended family or who live a great distance from them. Friends are a special lifeline, as well, for women whose husbands work long hours or travel a great deal.

Every mom at home benefits when she has two kinds of peer support: close personal friends and an organization for moms at home.

Close Friends. Every woman at home needs at least three to five close women friends. These are women she can share with at an emotionally intimate level and with whom she can be herself. She can cry with them, if need be, or call on them in emergencies. She doesn't need to clean her house before they come over; and she doesn't expect them to clean for her either.

Close friendships don't spring up overnight. They are deliberately cultivated over time. Christian women have an advantage, in that they already share a common spiritual bond with each other that facilitates growing closer emotionally. At-home moms who are new in town and those who have recently quit work to stay at home must put forth effort to make friends with other women who choose to be at home. Pray for God's direction in developing these friendships because these relationships are so vital to a successful season at home.

One way to meet like-minded women is through a support group for mothers at home.

Organized Support. Many community groups exist for mothers at home. Many churches also offer mother's clubs and groups such as MOPS (Mothers of Preschoolers). My church sponsors a mothers group called Helpmate. This group began several years ago when some at-home moms felt the need for older women in the church to serve as mentors, helping younger mothers raise their children.

Helpmate is now attended by women from several local churches. Mothers enjoy a time of fellowship and refreshments, offer each other prayer support in small groups, and then gather for a teaching time or to hear a speaker. Child care is provided for a nominal amount. One of the chief benefits of a group like Helpmate is that it provides that much-needed avenue for meeting other mothers at home and for cultivating friendships with them.

Many of the women I surveyed are active in this particular group. "Helpmate has been a gift from God," said Shannon. "I spent many years at home alone and felt like an island to myself. Helpmate has brought me together with like-minded mothers and given me a place to share my hopes and fears . . . a magnificent blessing to me!" Bonny said, "It's provided lots of new information and helped me form lasting friendships."

Holly appreciates the support she receives: "It is so encouraging to be with mothers who are in the same boat. It diminishes loneliness. It is very helpful for exchanging ideas. I learn a lot from the speakers and it gives me that much-needed intellectual stimulation." Amy concurred: "It is a tremendous support to share the trials and joys of raising children with other like-minded women. Also, the insights of older mentors help encourage and teach us new mothers."

SURVIVAL KIT ITEM #3:
GIVE PRIORITY TO YOUR MARRIAGE

Unless she is independently wealthy, no married woman can spend a season at home with her children without both financial and emotional support from her husband. His financial support is essential because a season at home, by definition, requires that the mother's focus be primarily on the children and not on earning income. (Even work-at-home moms assign their home business a lower priority than the children.) Emotionally, a husband's support is necessary so that the mother can give herself wholly to her mothering with the knowledge that her husband is behind her efforts.

Support from Husbands: Survey Results. The majority of the women in my survey said they would describe their husbands as enthusiastic about having them stay at home with the children. "My husband's enthusiastic support is the single greatest factor that got me through a difficult first year with my son," said Kris. "Our marriage has grown tremendously because of this. There has never been a conflict between us because I stayed home, only conflicts we faced as a team, like changes in financial status."

Carol said that her husband's support makes her marriage stronger and her mothering more worthwhile. Sherry stated that having her husband's support "really helps because I know he feels that what I am doing is important." Said Patti, "I don't feel so guilty about not being a Super Mom and trying to handle career with family, knowing he's behind me 100 percent."

A few of the women surveyed said their husbands gave reluctant support to their decision to be at home. In every case, this seemed to stem from the pinch of finances. Shannon described her husband as reluctant, even though she said that her husband would not describe himself that way. She perceives that his reluctance is due to financial concerns. "So," she said, "I struggle to make money at home to please him." Bonny said her husband is both enthusiastic and reluctant. He is entirely in favor of Bonny being at home with the children but concerned about the financial difficulty it causes the family.

After Kate started staying at home, she saw her husband's attitude change from reluctant to supportive. "My husband was reluctant when I first wanted to quit and become a full-time mom," she related. "Now he says he enjoys having me at home and would not want me to return to work. His enthusiastic support has been essential to my continuing to be a full-time mom. It was very difficult for me when I felt I needed to constantly prove my worthiness as a full-time mom."

Couple Time. One of the difficulties couples often face during a season at home is finding time away from children to nurture their marriage. Since a tight budget often goes hand in hand with a season at home, coming up with money for dates and baby-sitters is also a common problem. I asked the women in my survey how they handle these obstacles to couple time.

There were two common strategies for finding time together. The first method was to put the children to bed early enough to still have time for each other. Paula described how she and her husband use this strategy regularly: "My husband and I get the kids in bed by 8:00 p.m. and generally spend a couple hours after that alone together. We've always talked a lot, and we try to pray together frequently and share our days with each other."

Several women mentioned another strategy: setting aside time for dates. Dee said, "My husband and I date about two times a month." The cost of child care was avoided either by getting relatives to baby-sit, as Bonny and her husband do, or by using Wendy's strategy. "We don't have family nearby, so baby-sitting gets expensive," she explained. "I'm planning on trading Friday nights with my neighbors, rotating to provide child care for each other." Those who could afford it added in more expensive getaways. Kate said that once or twice a year she and her husband take trips without the children. Dee and her husband go away for a weekend every three months.

Equal Down Time for Dads. After a tough day, it is tempting to pass the kids off to dad the moment he comes through the door and head straight for a bubble bath. Remember, however, that your husband needs time to recharge, regroup, and be alone, just as you do. Some men find that between work and dad duty, every waking moment is spoken for. Discuss with your husband his need for down time and work out a compromise that will allow both of you to have some time to yourselves each day. Some families find that when dad can have the first twenty to thirty minutes after he gets home all to himself, he will be more enthusiastic about giving his wife a break from the kids.

SURVIVAL KIT ITEM #4:
CULTIVATE A STRONG WALK WITH GOD

Many women who responded to my survey said that they and their husbands had chosen a season at home because they had a strong sense that this is what God wanted them to do. Some stepped out in obedience to what they understood God's will to be, in spite of financial and other difficulties. As they did, they brought to life the truth of 1 Thessalonians 5:24: "The one who calls you is faithful and he will do it."

Once a woman comes home for a season, she often finds herself at a new, unexpected juncture in her walk with God. Like every relationship, a relationship with God requires an investment of time. Spending time reading the Bible, we discover who God is as he speaks to us through his Word. Spending time in prayer, we reveal our thoughts, desires, and needs to God. As we nurture this relationship over time, intimacy with God develops.

To draw strength and wisdom for each day's dilemmas and decisions, full-time mothers must stay connected to God. During a season at home, however, many mothers discover that the lack of any time to themselves is a hindrance to spiritual growth.

It takes both diligence and creativity to overcome the obstacles to maintaining a close walk with God during the years at home. (God, of course, understands what moms at home are up against!) Here are some strategies that moms at home employ in maintaining their relationship with God.

1. Instead of reading a chapter of Scripture each day, choose a few verses, or just one verse, to meditate on throughout the day. Some women like to write the verse on an index card and keep it in view as they go about the day's tasks.

2. Instead of reading Scripture, listen to it. Record passages of Scripture onto cassette tapes and listen to them on a Walkman as you do housework or exercise. You can also purchase a copy of the Bible on tape.

3. Instead of one formal time with God, maintain fellowship all day long by praying on the run—in the car, between loads of laundry, and at odd moments during the day. Let a frequent task be a reminder to pray. For example, every time you unload the dishwasher or nurse a baby or change a diaper, pray for those who eat meals with you or for the child you are caring for. When some women iron they pray for the family member whose garment they are pressing.

4. Find a prayer partner with whom you are comfortable praying over the phone. Nap times or early mornings are good times to connect with your prayer partner.

5. Select Bible verses to memorize with your children. This nourishes both of you spiritually and provides a common bond as well.

6. Play or sing Christian music in your house and car. Whether you like contemporary music or classic hymns, songs with a Christian message sweeten the atmosphere while embedding truth into minds and hearts.

7. It is also helpful to meditate upon God's character, as evidenced by the various names mentioned throughout Scripture. Some of God's names have special meaning for at-home moms. He is *Jehovah-Jireh*, the God who provides (Genesis 22:14). He is *El-Olam*, the eternally existent one, who never changes (Genesis 21:33). He is *El Shaddai*, the giver of strength (Genesis 17:1-4). And he is *Jehovah Shalom*, the Lord our peace (Judges 6:24).

No matter what the need may be—financial provision, supportive friends, emotional comfort, wisdom, direction, strength and energy, or peace—mothers who walk with God find him to be an endless resource and an ever-present ally.

SURVIVAL KIT ITEM #5: CULTIVATE A SENSE OF HUMOR

Surviving a season at home, in large measure, means surviving emotionally. That's why finding the funny in the adventures and misadventures of life with kids is so important. Life seems less heavy when garnished with humor. The load seems lighter, and domestic disasters are less likely to be blown out of proportion. Every mom at home needs a well-honed sense of humor in her survival kit.

Mothers who can draw upon their sense of humor at opportune moments model for their children a healthy approach to life. Children tend to filter their perceptions through the emotional ambiance created by their mothers. If mom shrieks and yells about both major and minor faux pas and problems, her children will probably respond by walking on eggshells and approaching life very seriously. But moms who can lighten up free their kids to do the same.

A mother's laughter and smiles bring relief to a child at a tense or difficult moment. And those special moms who are uninhibited enough to really have fun with their kids— to giggle and get down on the floor and be silly—give their children a wonderful, memorable gift.

If humor doesn't come naturally to you, or when life really is more difficult than funny, it may be helpful to import some humor. Buy a joke book and swap jokes with your kids. Subscribe to the *Reader's Digest* or *Christian Parenting Today* and read the anecdotes from readers out loud at the dinner table. Buy a silly songs tape or silly rhymes book or make up your own silly poems. Be creative—but make life at your house fun!

SURVIVAL KIT ITEM #6:
STAY IN TOUCH WITH YOUR PROFESSION

You may already have plans to return to work when your children reach a certain age. If you do, you understand the importance of keeping in touch with your profession. But even if you plan to be at home for many years (or permanently), keeping in touch with your profession is still a good idea. Why? Because even though your heart is at home and your plans are made, there may be events ahead which you can neither foresee nor control. While it is unpleasant to think about circumstances that could force you back to work, it is prudent to do so. If your husband should lose his job or pass away unexpectedly, if he were to become disabled, or if your marriage came to an end, you might find yourself back on the job market. Would you be prepared?

Here are some ways to maintain a grip on your profession during the at-home season:

1. Read books pertaining to your area of expertise. Set a goal: can you read two a year? (Settle for one if you have to.)

2. If your profession has an association (for example, the Society of Manufacturing Engineers), attend the meetings at least occasionally. Meetings are scheduled in advance (and usually printed in the newsletter, if there is one), so you can arrange for child care ahead of time. If you are not sure whether your profession has an association, consult the *Encyclopedia of Associations* in your public library.

3. Take a refresher course. This is especially important if your profession requires a current license or certification in order to work (such as teaching, nursing, or selling real estate).

4. Subscribe to any professional newsletters or magazines that will keep you abreast of trends in your field.

5. Volunteer for a few hours a month. This keeps your skills sharp and allows you to learn new ones. Think of volunteering as a practicum that increases your expertise but costs you nothing.

6. Stay in touch with former co-workers. Periodically phone them or meet them for lunch.

When, or if, the time arrives for you to return to work outside your home, you can enhance your job opportunities by preparing a great resumé. Some employment counselors suggest that you can put your best foot forward by arranging your resumé according to function, rather than chronology. This will call attention to your skills rather than the time you spent at home. Your public library has books that can help you put together an outstanding resumé. The Association of Part-Time Professionals also offers a step-by-step guide called *Sure-Hire Resumés*. (Call for current price: 704-734-7975.)

SURVIVAL KIT ITEM #7: KNOW WHY YOU'RE HOME

The mothers I surveyed were more than happy to tell me why they chose to be at home with their children for a season.

Sherry said, "The thing that makes it worthwhile to me is just knowing I'm doing the best thing, in my opinion, for my child." According to Karen, the most important things were, "Knowing I can be here when my family needs me, seeing all the 'firsts,' and not feeling torn between work and home priorities." Patti said the best thing was, "Being totally loved by two adorable kids who think I'm great."

"The best thing about being at home is seeing the contentment on my child's face and having him express his appreciation and love for me and all I do for him," said Holly. "It's wonderful to have a very close relationship with your child." For Kathie, the best thing was knowing that she was "providing something for my children that money cannot buy."

How about you? If you are an at-home mom, do you know exactly why you are at home? A clear sense of why we're doing what we're doing helps us keep on keeping on when the going gets rough. Take a sheet of paper and see if you can put your convictions about full-time mothering into words. If what comes out on the paper reflects what is in your heart, post your "mother's manifesto" where you will see it often.

If you are considering a season at home, putting your thoughts on paper may help you as well. Why are you considering coming home? Why does it seem worth your consideration? What will you gain and how will your family benefit if you decide in favor of a season at home? As part of your "decision manifesto," you might want to include the

181

advantages and disadvantages of a season at home for your particular family.

NO GUARANTEES

Staying at home, in and of itself, provides no guarantee of anything. What a mother does with her time and how she connects emotionally with her children is what makes a season at home valuable. It is possible for a mother to stay at home full-time and be emotionally or physically unavailable to her children. Work-at-home moms need to be mindful of the importance of staying tuned in to their children's needs and feelings.

Serious problems such as depression, marital conflict, or dependency on alcohol or drugs can effectively remove a mother from her children. Her body may be at home, but she may as well be somewhere else. Emotionally, her children feel abandoned.

Children who grow up feeling emotionally abandoned often experience significant personal problems as adults. Therefore, it is critical for mothers who struggle with serious problems to get appropriate professional help. The right kind of therapy can help them recover and begin to be available to their kids during a season at home. Remember that getting help is a sign of wisdom, not weakness. Don't hesitate to seek help for yourself and your family if you know it is needed.

Over-commitment can also impair the quality of a season at home. Well-meaning mothers can over-commit to a variety of things, even necessities like housework, or stress-relievers like crafts or tennis. Many full-time mothers find that they are in great demand. They are recruited to volunteer in the community, in the church, at school, and in the neighborhood. These volunteer responsibilities sometimes add up to more time away from home than a part-time job would require. And children who are shuffled from nursery to nursery and sitter to sitter because of mom's many commitments are no better off than if their mothers were not at home. In a sense, these children are abandoned too.

If you've come home for a season, remember why you're there! Certainly every mom at home will do her share of laundry and cooking. Hopefully every mom at home will find time for lunching with friends, volunteering, and enjoying creative outlets. Some moms will work at home too. But no matter what your responsibilities and creative outlets are, never lose sight of the fact that your children are the reason for a season at home.

ELEVEN

Five Loaves and Two Fish

Probably of anything we've ever done in our whole lives, my quitting work was the strongest act of faith.

—Mary Howe, thirty-three, mother of three

Is a season at home God's will for every family? For yours? In chapter one, we examined the paradigm of sequencing from the perspective of stewardship. We said that as mothers, we had been made stewards not only of our children, but of our own talents and abilities as well. We admitted that in the fast-paced, unstable culture of the nineties, good stewardship is a complicated thing. We also noted that because stewardship is an individual responsibility, it can never be "one size fits all." We observed, as well, that individual stewardship implies diversity, not sameness.

So what do you think: Is a season at home God's will for every family? For yours?

GOD'S WILL

I don't believe that any of us can determine with any degree of certainty whether a season at home is or is not God's will for another family. It may or may not be part of God's plan for a particular family, in their individual circumstances, at a particular point in time. That is to say, as outsiders, we can never determine God's *specific* will for other people.

But what we can do is make an observation about the *general* will of God. We can say that a season at home does not conflict with the general will of God. Or, to put it another way, in general, a season at home finds favor with God.

How can we say this? Because in Scripture we find the revealed, general will of God. And, to the best of my knowledge, there is nothing in Scripture that cautions against or counsels against a season at home. On the contrary, we can find scriptural support for a season at home.

Three passages which I believe lend credence to the idea of a season at home are quoted below. (The italics are added to call attention to significant phrases.)

Titus 2:3–5. In this passage Paul was elaborating upon what he termed in verse one as "fitting for sound doctrine" (NASB). In verses 3-5 he instructs the older women to "encourage the young women to love their husbands, to *love their children,* to be sensible, pure, *workers at home,* kind, being subject to their own husbands, that the word of God may not be dishonored" (NASB).

Psalm 113:9. "He [God] settles the barren woman *in her home* as a *happy mother* of children." The *New American Standard Bible* uses the phrase, "a *joyful* mother of children."

1 Timothy 5:14. In the context of instructing the church about how to care for its widows, Paul said, "I counsel younger widows to marry, to have children, *to manage their homes* and to give the enemy no opportunity for slander."

GOD'S HAND IN A SEASON AT HOME

In surveying and interviewing mothers at home, I was especially curious about how these women perceived God's role in their decision to come home for a season. How did the very practical matters of a season at home intertwine with their faith? Had they sensed in any way that God was calling them home? Could they point to ways in which God had provided for them financially or materially? I asked, and I learned a lot.

These mothers at home tutored me in some very practical matters. But I was most excited by what I learned from them about the way things work in the spiritual realm.

Sometimes God Calls Mothers to a Season at Home

Rebecca fully intended to return to work after the birth of her baby, but God intervened in her plans. "During my pregnancy," she said, "God seemed to be nudging me to be a stay-at-home mom. God seemed to be telling me that my daughter would need me more than anyone at work would. It seemed that every article, newscast, and radio program was directed straight at me. I felt very confused to be having these feelings."

As related in chapter seven, Rebecca and her husband reevaluated their plans and Rebecca stayed at home with their baby daughter. What I learned from Rebecca was that comprehending God's call can, at first, feel confusing.

Kate worked full-time for several years when her first two children were young. She says, "I enjoyed my job and was a little afraid of staying home." But she began to feel strongly that her place was at home with her children. Her husband disagreed with the idea of Kate quitting work. He told her she would be wasting her education and experience. Kate related how God worked in their situation:

> I prayed for months. I was feeling very frustrated that the Lord did not seem to be guiding me. Finally, I prayed that the Lord would show me by that October

187

whether, financially, I would be able to leave my job, and whether leaving a job I enjoyed was what he wanted me to do.

Within a few weeks of this prayer, my husband was offered a new job, which meant relocating to another city, and a substantial raise. And the date he was to report for the new position was—October first!

With the move and the raise, Kate was able to stay at home with her children (she now has three). According to Kate, her husband now likes having her at home and would not want her to return to work.

What I learned from Kate was this: Acknowledge the desires of your heart, even when you feel a bit afraid and those closest to you feel differently. Pray about your desires and wait patiently for God's answer.

After a Decision Is Made, the Ante May Go Up

A couple determined to have a season at home may be tested: How strong are their convictions? Can they be bought if the price is right?

Pam, thirty-five, is currently an at-home mother of two. But six years ago, when she first learned she was pregnant, Pam almost decided to become a working mom. Here is her story.

Pam worked in corporate management. "I had a good career and enjoyed using my skills and abilities," she explained. "I also got some measure of my self-worth from my job." After seven years in her career, Pam discovered that she was pregnant.

Pam remembers feeling sure that God wanted her to stay at home with her baby. She and her husband made plans for Pam to resign from her position and come home to raise their family. Pam was ready for this step. "After seven years in the corporate world, I realized that the stress, attitudes, and atmosphere of it all was not worth it," she said. "There really was not the fulfillment in a career that the world says there is." But then came what Pam described as the tough part.

"While pregnant and planning to quit," Pam said, "I was offered a position as a vice president." This was quite an honor—Pam would have been the first woman vice president in her division. It also would have brought a pay raise of $10,000 a year.

Pam admitted, "I was tempted to take it." She began to reason with herself, making a case for continuing to work until she had a second child. Then, said Pam, "I realized all the reasons I already had for staying home had not changed, and I was convinced God wanted me at home, so I turned it down."

Looking back, Pam regarded her exodus from corporate life this way: "God is faithful. I was given an assistant vice president title before quitting. Just a title—no increase in salary. But still the first female officer. I believe God honored my decision then and is still doing so." If she had it to do over, would she do anything differently? Pam responded, "I have never once regretted turning down what I was offered."

I learned from Pam that God's leading doesn't necessarily change in the face of a bigger paycheck.

Long before we ask, God knows what we need and when we will need it. He may have the answers to our prayers waiting in the wings. When we begin to pray, God may begin to set his plan into motion. When he does, it can seem like a coincidence.

Remember Rebecca? Here's the story behind the decision Rebecca and her husband made: "I took our situation to the Lord in prayer and, seemingly coincidentally (although I know better), my husband was offered a position with a new company. The salary was considerably higher, allowing us to adjust more easily to the financial burdens. God is so good. My husband was not searching for another job when this opportunity fell into his lap. It definitely was a God-send. He saw the desire of my heart and made good on his promise."

Kris had a similar experience. She was home on

maternity leave trying to determine whether they would be able to meet their financial obligations if she quit work. "I didn't want to make a hasty decision about whether to go back to work," she said. So that she and her husband could take their time in deciding, her husband's parents sent the young family two hundred dollars a month for the first four or five months.

"Then," said Kris, "my boss called." He told her that the company was reducing its work force and that Kris was eligible for a separation package. "This package (which I gladly took) provided me with a $12,000 check and 100 percent benefits for an additional year," Kris explained.

Looking back on the circumstances that opened the door to her season at home, Kris said, "I firmly believe God and God alone provided this money for us."

I learned two things from Kris and Rebecca: God does provide, often in surprising ways, in response to the trust and petitions of his children, and it is important to recognize the hand of God in our blessings, giving him the honor and glory when things work out.

As encouraging as Kris and Rebecca's experiences are, we must remember that God usually provides for a season at home in ordinary ways. Kathie's story illustrates this truth:

> When I became pregnant with our first child, I was the support of our family by working forty hours a week while my husband was a graduate student. We lived in an apartment and had one car and an income of fifteen thousand dollars in the expensive culture of Southern California. We prayed a lot about my staying home with our baby.
>
> By the time my maternity leave expired, my husband was working part-time, earning enough to match my salary. There were no frills in our life, but we paid our bills and I stayed home. We believed, and still believe, that relationships are more important than things.
>
> When my husband's graduation came, our goal was to live somewhere that would allow us to buy our

first house and for me to stay home. The Lord opened the door which provided for both. The house wasn't new and it wasn't in a fancy neighborhood, but he met our need. I believe that when our goal is to honor him, he will provide for us.

The usual path to a season at home is the one Kathie and her husband journeyed. What I learned from Kathie is, in her own words, "When our goal is to honor God, he will provide for us."

FAITH FOR THE SEASON

When the family financial picture looks bleak, a couple may begin to weigh their material resources against those of other families they know. A comparative lack of cash may prompt them to wonder: Could this be a sign that we are not supposed to pursue a season at home? Is a season at home part of God's plan for our family?

Measuring our circumstances against those of others is a mistake. We are all at different places on the journey between the cradle and our heavenly home. If we feel the pinch of finances, it may be because God knows it will prompt us to give him our full attention. Chances are, he's trying to teach us something important.

Bear in mind also that a God-given desire for a season at home does not always make sense financially. If we look only at the family checkbook, a season at home may seem a most illogical or imprudent undertaking. Parents may gaze long and hard at their own "five loaves and two fish" and question, as the disciples once did, how so little could possibly be stretched to meet so many needs.

A season at home would be a shoo-in for any family, if they could just win the Publisher's Clearinghouse Sweepstakes or inherit a fortune at the reading of Great-Aunt Bessie's will or be offered an unbelievably high-paying job. I've noticed, however, that in most cases, God withholds such lightening bolts of divine provision.

Receiving these windfalls would open the door to a

season at home, but stepping across the threshold would require no faith. We would see at the outset where our provision was coming from. What God cherishes, and therefore seeks to cultivate, is our trust in him. Faith grows well in a financial climate that forces us to trust God instead of our own ability to earn a living.

The desire for a season at home without the visible means to pull it off constitutes what the Bible calls a *trial*. The purpose of trials is not to make us miserable; the purpose of trials is to make us like Christ. Reflect on James 1:2-4: "Consider it pure joy, my brothers, whenever you face trials of many kinds, because you know that the testing of your faith develops perseverance. Perseverance must finish its work so that you may be mature and complete, not lacking anything." From an eternal perspective, trials are our greatest opportunities.

Do you desire a season at home? Do you wish that God would stockpile plenty of resources for you and place them where you could see them? If so, I nominate Proverbs 3:5-6 as your theme verses: "Trust in the Lord with all your heart and lean not on your own understanding; in all your ways acknowledge him, and he will make your paths straight."

It takes both trial and blessing to weave a tapestry of faith sufficient for a season at home. Only God is wise enough to choose the threads.

TWELVE

Carpe Diem

Carpe diem, quam minimum credula postero.
(Seize the day; put no trust in the morrow.)
—Horace, 65–8 B.C.

This is a book that took shape in my mind and heart over several years. It is, however, a book that I put off writing. For a long time, the whole topic of moms at work and moms at home appeared too controversial to tackle. Yet the more I researched and studied, the more my convictions grew, and the more convinced I became that this topic, while admittedly sticky, was tremendously important and worthy of my best efforts.

When I finally began writing, in an effort to underscore the strength of my sentiments, I penned the following words as part of what I envisioned to be a postscript:

> My earnest wish is that no one will dismiss the message
> of this book with the words, That's easy for *you* to say.
> But if they did, I would have to agree that it does appear
> easy for me to encourage women to set aside a season at
> home. My husband has a corporate job that allows me
> to continue to extend my at-home season into my son's
> school years. We own our home, and our needs are

amply met. I know, however, that all this could change tomorrow. . . .

Little did I realize how prophetic that last sentence was. Only a few weeks after I committed those thoughts to writing, the unthinkable happened: after sixteen years of marriage, my husband and I separated. Along with the shock, the hurt, and the sense of abandonment came the realization that overnight I had become a single parent. It was not my choice, but it has become my reality.

My days as a full-time, stay-at-home mom appear to be in jeopardy. I don't know what lies ahead. More than anything, I want to remain available to my child. My hope (and yes, I will dare to say, my expectation) is that God will make a way for me to work full-time at home—much as he has done for some of the women whose stories appear on the preceding pages.

What happened to me while writing this book cast a new light on what was an already heartfelt topic. As a result, I believe I was able to write with a broader perspective, having seen firsthand both sides of the philosophical fence that often divides moms at home from moms who work. I know what it is to have been at home with my child—to have had a choice—and I know what it means to have that choice threatened.

My enthusiasm for a season at home is well known. Completing this book while prayerfully and tearfully weighing career opportunities and work-at-home possibilities was one of the most ironic experiences of my life. In the wake of my personal crisis, friends have said to me, "If this can happen to you, then it can happen to anyone." I think they are right. And to any woman who longs for a season at home with her children and is in a position to exercise that option, my advice is, *carpe diem*.

Carpe diem is a Latin phrase meaning *seize the day*. The idea is that since we do not know what tomorrow will bring, we must make the most of today. Today is the only day any of us can be sure of. It is the only day we have, so we must take today's opportunities and make them count. The wisdom of this idea is affirmed by Ephesians 5:15–16, which says, "Be very careful, then, how you live—not as unwise but as wise, making the most of every opportunity, because the days are evil."

Not one of us knows what tomorrow will bring. Overnight, finances can change. Our health or the health of a family member can fail. And as unthinkable as it may be, marital status can also change. Divorce or the death of a spouse has changed the lives of many women and children, completely removing any possibility of a season at home.

A *carpe diem* mindset keeps the fragility and brevity of life before us. It helps us to live in the reality of the present and not in a fantasy of the future. It helps us cherish our children and live before God with gratitude. It helps ensure that the choices we make today are wise, reflecting our convictions.

The concept of *carpe diem* first became significant to me one sunny fall afternoon a few years ago when my son, Chris, was five. Our family was spending some time with friends who live in the country. They had arranged a special treat for the children—rides on a big horse named Pal. The children took turns on Pal's back as a grownup led him around the riding ring. It was great fun—until something startled Pal.

Outside the fence, I watched in horror as the huge animal broke into a gallop straight toward my son. I saw my little boy begin to run, but I knew his efforts would be futile. In a matter of seconds the fifteen-hundred-pound horse had run straight over Chris. I saw my son lying face down in the dirt.

My adrenaline was pumping furiously but everything seemed to move in eerie slow motion. I raced toward Chris. His daddy got there first and scooped him up in loving arms.

Chris could have been killed. One blow from a flying hoof could have left him brain damaged or maimed for life. But he wasn't injured. All four hooves had missed his body. Chris had tripped and fallen before Pal reached him, and he landed on the ground in such perfect alignment with the horse's path that he was untouched as the animal flew over his body. It still seems like a miracle.

Weeks later as I reflected on that experience, I knew that if my son had been killed, I would not have regretted one day of the years I had spent at home with him. In fact, those days would have been all the more precious and well-spent.

Now I consider my present circumstances the same way. As the author of a book about children and divorce,[1] I am painfully aware of the impact separation and divorce can have on my child. But I am also comforted, knowing that the stability and security of having had an at-home mom for an extended season has undergirded my son in ways which will now be of tremendous benefit to him. I regard having been at home with my child for the past eight years as a valuable investment which has prepared him for the changes that will now come into his life. While I could never have predicted or imagined the breakup of our family, God knew that day would come.

As I write these words, much about our family's future and my own employment is uncertain. No matter what lies ahead, I am thankful to have had the opportunity to be at home. Now, more than ever, it seems like time invested well. And as I look to the future, I know that if God in his kindness grants me a way to earn a living and remain at home, I will be unspeakably grateful.

If there is anything positive about the specter of personal crisis or tragedy, perhaps it is that our priorities are jolted into sharp focus. We look back in time and then forward and ask ourselves hard questions: What would we do differently if we had the chance? How do we feel about the choices we made in the past? If we could somehow know the future, would we make different choices in the present?

This book is written for mothers who have a choice about working or being at home. It is written as well for those who could, with effort, manipulate their circumstances to accommodate a season at home. The preceding chapters set forth many compelling reasons for setting aside a season at home. Yet to those mothers contemplating a season at home, I would also say this: possibly the best reason for choosing a season at home may simply be that today it is possible for you to choose it. Tomorrow it may not be. The time you can have with your children today may well be part of God's plan for equipping them for whatever he knows they will face in the years ahead.

Carpe Diem. Seize the day!

Appendix A

SURVEY RESULTS: THIRTY MOMS WHO FOUND A WAY

The mothers who responded to this survey did so on the basis of anonymity. In the text, survey respondents are referred to by pseudonym.

Age:

These mothers ranged in age from twenty-eight to forty-four. The average age was thirty-four.

Number of Children:

The thirty mothers surveyed had a combined total of sixty-five children. The average number of children per family was two. Largest number of children per family was four.

Ages of Children:

Children ranged in age from three months to thirteen years. The average age was five.

Education of Mothers:

High School Graduates: 5 (Shannon, Tara, April, Carol, Sandra)

College Graduates: 18 (Kelly, Patti, Bonny, Wendy, Dee, Kris, Sherry, Cami, Rebecca, Paula, Pam, Mary Ann, Holly, Kate, Lisa, Kerri, Meredith, Jan)

Graduate Study: 7 (Michelle, Melanie, Kathie, Amy, Charesa, Kelsey, Shelley)

Occupation Prior to Coming Home for a Season:

Amy:	learning disabilities teacher
April:	secretary
Bonny:	personal banker
Cami:	television production
Carol:	medical secretary
Charesa:	children's and preschool director on church staff
Dee:	teacher
Holly:	dental hygienist
Jan:	sales rep
Kate:	registered nurse
Kathie:	teacher, administrative assistant
Kelly:	social worker, day-care worker
Kelsey:	teacher
Kerri:	nurse
Kris:	banking and sales
Lisa:	ICU nurse
Mary Ann:	elementary teacher
Melanie:	social worker, airline reservationist
Meredith:	banking
Michelle:	teacher
Pam:	actuarial, systems, and project manager
Patti:	registered nurse
Paula:	registered nurse
Rebecca:	teacher
Sandra:	airline reservationist
Shannon:	secretary
Shelley:	teacher
Sherry:	materials planning administrator
Tara:	medical secretary
Wendy:	nurse

Present Family Income:

Family incomes ranged from between $15,000-$25,000 a year to over $100,000. Seven families had an income of less than $35,000 a year. Ten family incomes were between $35,000 and $55,000. Eleven families made more than $55,000 a year. Two women did not disclose their family income.

Breakdown:

$15,000-$25,000	Kelly
$25,000-$35,000	Patti, Shannon, Bonny, Wendy, Sandra, April
$35,000-$45,000	Dee, Kris, Michelle, Carol, Lisa
$45,000-$55,000	Sherry, Cami, Melanie, Rebecca, Meredith
$55,000-$65,000	Paula, Kathie, Kelsey
$65,000-$75,000	Pam, Shelley
$75,000-$85,000	Tara, Mary Ann
$85,000-$100,000	Holly, Amy
over $100,000	Charesa, Kate

Income not disclosed: Kerri, Jan

Appendix B

RESOURCES FOR A SEASON AT HOME

For Stay-at-Home Mothers:

Books

Staying Home: From Full-Time Professional to Full-Time Parent, by Darcie Sanders & Martha M. Bullen (Boston: Little, Brown & Co., 1992).

Sequencing: Having It All but Not All at Once, by Arlene Rossen Cardozo (New York: Atheneum, 1986).

Home by Choice, by Brenda Hunter, Ph.D. (Portland, Ore.: Multnomah, 1991).

How to Really Love Your Child, by Dr. Ross Campbell (Wheaton, Ill.: Victor Books, 1977).

A Parent's Guide to the First Three Years of Life, by Burton L. White (New York: Prentice-Hall, 1980).

Support Groups

F.E.M.A.L.E. (Formerly Employed Mothers
   at the Leading Edge)
P.O. Box 31
Elmhurst, IL 60126
708-941-3553

Offers a monthly newsletter and has local chapters across the country (annual membership: $20).

MOPS International (Mothers of Preschoolers)
1311 South Clarkson Street
Denver, CO 80210
303-733-5353

A SEASON AT HOME

A Christ-centered ministry for mothers of infants through kindergartners which offers a monthly newsletter and chartered groups in churches across the country.

Mothers At Home
8310A Old Courthouse Road
Vienna, VA 22182
1-800-783-4MOM

Offers a forum for at-home moms via its monthly magazine, *Welcome Home* (one-year subscription: $15) and represents mothers at home to the media and government.

La Leche League
800-LA LECHE (800-525-3243)

Provides information and support for breast-feeding moms and a bi-monthly magazine: *New Beginnings* (subscription: $15).

Mothers of Twins
P.O. Box 23188
Albuquerque, NM 87192-1188
505-275-0955

Offers local support groups and newsletter, an annual convention, and a quarterly notebook.

For Living on Less:

The Tightwad Gazette: Promoting Thrift as a Viable Alternative Lifestyle, by Amy Dacyczyn (New York: Villard Books: 1993).

The Tightwad Gazette
RR1
Box 3570
Leeds, ME 04263

A one-year subscription to this newsletter is $12.

Consumer Information Catalog
R. Woods
Consumer Information Center-3A
P.O. Box 100
Pueblo, CO 81002

This free catalog offers pamphlets such as "Nine Ways to Lower Your Auto Insurance," "How to Buy Surplus Personal Property from the Dept. of Defense," and "Growing Vegetables in the Home Garden." It may be available at your library. Some pamphlets have a nominal cost.

Resolution Trust Corporation
800-RTC-3006 (800-782-3006)

Provides information on items such as real estate, furniture, cars, and computers offered for auction across the country and in specified zip code areas.

For Working at Home:

Books

1001 Businesses You Can Start From Home: The World's Most Complete Directory of Part-Time and Full-Time Business Ideas, Including Start-up Costs, Marketing Tips, Sources of Information, by Daryl Allen Hall (New York: John Wiley & Sons, Inc., 1992).

The Work-at-Home Sourcebook: How To Find "At Home" Work That's Right for You, by Lynie Arden (Boulder, Colo.: Live Oak Publications, 1987).

How to Sell Your Homemade Creations, by Alan Smith (Lakeland, Fla.: Success Publishing Company).

Homemade Money, by Barbara Brabec (Crozet, Va.: Betterway Publications, 1987). This book is $18.95 at your local bookstore, or send $21.95 to P.O. Box 2137, Naperville, IL 60567.

Working from Home: Everything You Need to Know about Living and Working under the Same Roof, by Paul and Sarah Edwards (Los Angeles: Jeremy P. Tarcher, Inc., 1990).

The Woman's Work-at-Home Handbook: Income and Independence with a Computer, by Patricia McConnel (New York: Bantam Books, 1986).

Periodicals and Newsletters

Home Business Success Catalog
P.O. Box 2137
Naperville, IL 60567
    This publication is free.

Home Office Computing magazine
740 Broadway
New York, NY 10003
    A one-year subscription is $19.97

Entrepreneur: The Small Business Authority
2392 Morse Avenue
Irvine, CA 92714

New Business Opportunities: The Business Start-Up Magazine
2392 Morse Avenue
Irvine, CA 92714

Working Options
Crescent Plaza
Suite 216
7700 Leesburg Pike
Falls Church, VA 22043
703-734-7975
    A newsletter published by the Association of Part-Time Professionals.

National Home Business Report
P.O. Box 2137
Naperville, IL 60567
    A one-year subscription to this quarterly newsletter is $24.

Consumer Information Catalog
P.O. Box 2137
Naperville, IL 60567
    Offers pamphlets such as, "Starting and Managing a Business from Your Home," "Guide to Business Credit for Women, Minorities, and Small Businesses," and "Financial Management: How to Make a Go of Your Business."

Appendix B

Other Resources

For Start-Up Information:

U.S. Small Business Administration Answer Desk
Washington, D.C.
800-827-5722

For Information on Benefits and Services for Work-at-Home Business People:

The National Business Association
800-456-0440

The National Independent Business League
800-683-0575

Part-Timer's Resource Kit
The Association of Part-Time Professionals
703-734-7975

Notes

Chapter 1: Paradigms

1. Kevin J. Williams et al., "Multiple Role Juggling and Daily Mood States in Working Mothers: An Experience Sampling Study," *Journal of Applied Psychology* 76, no. 5 (1991): 665.
2. Edith Fierst, "Careers and Kids," *Ms.* (May 1988): 62–64.

Chapter 2: A Season at Home

1. Brian E. Vaughn, Frederick L. Gove, and Byron Egeland, "The Relationship between Out-of-Home Care and the Quality of Infant Mother Attachment in an Economically Disadvantaged Population," *Child Development* 51 (1980): 1203–14.
2. Pamela Schwartz, "Length of Day Care Attendance and Attachment Behavior in Eighteen-Month-Old Infants," *Child Development* 54 (1983): 1073–78.
3. Ron Haskins, "Public Varying Day-Care Experience," *Child Development* 56 (1985): 689–703.
4. Paul Lutkenhaus, Klaus E. Grossmann, and Karin Grossmann, "Infant-Mother Attachment at Twelve Months and Style of Interaction with a Stranger at the Age of Three Years," *Child Development* 56 (1985): 1538–42.
5. Peter Barglow, Brian E. Vaughn, and Nancy Molitor, "Effects of Maternal Absence Due to Employment on the Quality of Infant-Mother Attachment in a Low-Risk Sample," *Child Development* 58 (1987): 945–54.
6. Carolee Howes, "Can the Age of Entry into Child Care and the Quality of Child Care Predict Adjustment in Kindergarten?" *Developmental Psychology* 26 (1990): 292–303.
7. Jay Belsky and Julia M. Braungart, "Are Insecure Infants with Extensive Day-Care Experience Less Stressed by and More Independent in the Strange Situation?" *Child Development* 62 (1991): 567–71.

8. Jay Belsky, "Infant Day Care: A Cause for Concern?" *Zero to Three: Bulletin of the National Center for Clinical Infant Programs* (Special Reprint): 5.

9. Kenneth Labich, "Can Your Career Hurt Your Kids?" *Fortune* (May 20, 1991): 40.

10. Ibid., 40–43.

11. Jay Belsky, "Parental and Nonparental Child Care and Children's Socioemotional Development: A Decade in Review," *Journal of Marriage and the Family* 52 (November 1990): 895.

12. Williams et al., "Multiple Role Juggling," 664.

13. *The Ryrie Study Bible* (Chicago: Moody Press, 1978), 1337 (note on Hosea 2:19).

14. Burton L. White, "Should You Stay Home With Your Baby?" *American Baby* (October 1985): 27.

15. Brenda Hunter, "Homeward Bound," *Focus on the Family* (January 1992): 7.

16. Claudia Wallis, "Is Day Care Bad for Babies?" *Time* (June 22, 1987): 63.

17. Burton L. White, *A Parent's Guide to the First Three Years of Life* (Englewood Cliffs, N.J.: Prentice-Hall, Inc, 1980), 2.

18. White, "Should You Stay Home?" 27.

19. Ross Campbell, "Parents Q & A," *Christian Parenting Today* (March/April 1991): 76.

20. White, *A Parent's Guide*, 36–37.

21. Ibid., 18.

22. Urie Bronfenbrenner, quoted by La Leche League International in "Excerpts from Literature Dealing with Mother-Baby Separation."

23. White, "Should You Stay Home?" 30.

24. Joyce Brothers, quoted by La Leche League International in "Excerpts from Literature Dealing with Mother-Baby Separation."

25. White, "Should You Stay Home?" 30.

26. Ibid.

Chapter 3: Changing Seasons

1. Joan Beck, *How To Raise a Brighter Child: The Case for Early Learning* (New York: Pocket Books, 1975), 31.

2. Dr. David Elkind, *The Hurried Child: Growing Up Too Fast Too Soon* (Reading, Mass.: Addison-Wesley, 1988), 152.

3. Connaught Marshner, "Is Day Care Good For Kids?" *National Review* (May 13, 1988): 30.

Notes

4. Kenneth Labich, "Can Your Career Hurt Your Kids?" *Fortune* (May 20, 1991): 52.
5. James C. Dobson and Gary Bauer, "Traditional Families: Fading or Flourishing?" *Focus on the Family* (May 1991): 8.

Chapter 4: Sequencing

1. Karyl E. MacEwen and Julius Barling, "Effects of Maternal Employment Experiences on Children's Behavior via Mood, Cognitive Difficulties, and Parenting Behavior," *Journal of Marriage and the Family* 53 (August 1991): 642.
2. Ibid., 635.
3. Ross Campbell, *How to Really Love Your Child* (Wheaton: Victor Books, 1977).
4. Sue Shellenbarger, "Flexible Policies May Slow Women's Careers" *Wall Street Journal* (Wednesday, April 22, 1992): B1.
5. Labich, "Can Your Career Hurt Your Kids?" 44.
6. Alice Kalso, "Family News," *Christian Parenting Today* (September/October 1990): 82.
7. Kathleen McCoy, "Is Your Child Flirting with Sex?" *Reader's Digest* (September 1989): 114.
8. Elkind, *The Hurried Child*, 137.

Chapter 5: Eight Good Reasons

1. The Associated Press, "Study: Hours at Work Increasing," *Winston-Salem Journal* (February 17, 1992): 1.
2. Brian Knowles, "Job vs. Family: Striking a Balance" *Focus on the Family* (June 1991): 2–4.
3. Linda Castrone, "Author Says Society Must Take Blame for Children's Woes," *Winston-Salem Journal* (August 3, 1991).
4. Julia Lawlor, "Suit Puts Spotlight on 'Daddy Stress,'" *USA Today* (June 21, 1991): 1B.
5. Carol Hymowitz, "Trading Fat Paychecks for Free Time," *Wall Street Journal* (August 5, 1991): B1.
6. Barbara Reynolds, "Job Success Can Mean Failure in Marriage," *USA Today* (Thursday, April 2, 1987): 11A.
7. Christopher Quinn, "Father's Heart Aches for Son," *Winston-Salem Journal* (April 10, 1992): 1.
8. Ellen Goodman, "Parents Need to Know When to Say No," *Winston-Salem Journal* (August 17, 1991): 12.
9. Dean Merrill and Mike Yorkey, "Focus at Fifteen," *Focus on the Family* (March 1992): 12.

10. Frank Tursi, "Children in Day Care Centers Must Fight Many Infections," *Winston-Salem Journal* (February 23, 1986): B2.
11. Frank Tursi, "Unhealthy?" *Winston-Salem Journal* (February 23, 1986): B1.
12. MacEwen and Barling, "Effects of Maternal Employment on Children's Behavior," 635-644.
13. Ibid.
14. Thomas F. O'Boyle, "Fast Track Kids Exhaust Their Parents," *Wall Street Journal* (Wednesday, August 7, 1991): B1.
15. Carol Hymowitz, "So Much to Do, So Little Time," *Wall Street Journal* (August 5, 1991): B1.
16. Rebecca Piirto, "New Women's Revolution," *American Demographics* (April 1991): 6.
17. Elkind, *The Hurried Child*, 189.
18. Susan Jacoby, "Roots of Success," *Family Circle* (April 5, 1988): 1–7.
19. David H. Demo, "Parent-Child Relations: Assessing Recent Changes," *Journal of Marriage and the Family* 54 (February 1992): 116.

Chapter 6: No Higher Calling

1. Charles F. Stanley, "An Inspiring Example of a Godly Mother," *In Touch* (May 1988): 19.
2. Harold S. Kushner, "Biggest Mistake I Ever Made," *Reader's Digest* (July 1991): 71.

Chapter 7: Decisions

1. Arlene Rossen Cardozo, *Sequencing: Having It All but Not All at Once* (New York: Atheneum, 1986), 93.
2. Kenneth S. Wuest, *Studies in the Vocabulary of the Greek New Testament*, Word Studies from the Greek New Testament 3 (Grand Rapids: Eerdmans, 1973), 64.
3. Darcie Sanders and Martha M. Bullen, *Staying Home: From Full-Time Professional to Full-Time Parent* (Boston: Little, Brown and Company: 1992), 60.
4. Cardozo, *Sequencing*, 91.
5. Sue Monk Kidd, "And They *Both* Did," *Guideposts* (November 1992): 6–9.

Chapter 8: Mission Impossible? (Maybe Not!)

1. Amy Dacyczyn, *The Tightwad Gazette: Promoting Thrift as a Viable Alternative Lifestyle* (New York: Villard Books, 1993), 1–4.

2. Kenneth S. Wuest, *Hebrews in the Greek New Testament*, Word Studies in the Greek New Testament 2 (Grand Rapids: Eerdmans, 1973), 128.

3. Merrill F. Unger, *Unger's Bible Dictionary* (Chicago: Moody Press, 1966), 1103.

4. "Good Morning America," ABC-TV, February 10, 1993.

5. Sue Shellenbarger, "Job Costs Eat Up Second Paychecks," *Wall Street Journal* (April 22, 1992): B1.

6. Janice Gaston, "More and More, Day Care is Becoming Company Policy," *Winston-Salem Journal* (February 5, 1991): 26.

7. Sanders and Bullen, *Staying Home*, 26.

8. Amy Dacyczyn, *The Tightwad Gazette*, 24.

9. Ibid., 52.

Chapter 9: Working at Home

1. Cheri Fuller, "Ways For Moms to Make Money at Home," *Focus on the Family* (January 1991): 2.

2. Research reported by "Good Morning America," ABC-TV, Wednesday, February 10, 1993.

3. The Associated Press, "Working at Home Growing," *Winston-Salem Journal* (April 20, 1992): 18.

4. Sanders and Bullen, *Staying Home*, 11.

5. Ibid., 99.

6. Lynie Arden, *The Work-at-Home Sourcebook: How to Find "At Home" Work That's Right for You* (Boulder: Live Oak Publications, 1987), 129.

7. Bernadette Grey, "Good Morning America," ABC-TV, Wednesday, February 10, 1993.

8. Marilyn Elias, "Dad's Role Crucial to Caring Kids," *USA Today* (May 30, 1990): A1.

Chapter 10: Survival Kit

1. Kay Donahue Jennings, Vaughan Stagg, and Robin E. Connors, "Social Networks and Mothers' Interactions with Their Preschool Children," *Child Development* 62 (1991): 976.

Chapter 12: Carpe Diem

1. Debbie Barr, *Children of Divorce: Helping Kids When Their Parents Are Apart* (Grand Rapids: Zondervan, 1992).